HOLY COMMUNION
and other Liturgical Resources

圣餐与其他崇拜礼仪资源

English/Chinese Edition
中/英双语版

Based on *A Prayer Book for Australia* (1995)

First published in 2017
by Broughton Publishing Pty Ltd
32 Glenvale Crescent Mulgrave VIC 3170

Copyright © Broughton Publishing 2017

All rights reserved. No part of this publication may be reproduced, stored in a retrieval system or transmitted, in any form or by any means electronic, photocopying, recording or otherwise, without the prior written permission of the publisher.

Translation Committee: Rev Ben Wong (Chair),
Rev Joseph Shih, Rev John Zhang,
Rev Kian Gee Lim, Rev Yvonne Poon
Proof Reader: Rev Dr Chou Wee Pan
Coordinator: Rev Canon Robert Vun

Paperback ISBN 978–0–9807244–7–9
ebook ISBN 978-0-9807244-8-6

Contents
目录

Morning and Evening Prayer First Order	2
早祷和晚祷崇拜程序一	3
Morning and Evening Prayer Second Order	30
早祷和晚祷崇拜程序二	31
The Holy Communion Second Order	50
圣餐崇拜程序二	51
The Holy Communion Third Order	88
圣餐崇拜程序三	89
Holy Baptism Confirmation in Holy Communion	114
洗礼、坚信礼圣餐崇拜包括确信礼和接纳礼	115
A Service for Marriage Second Order	154
婚礼程序二	155
Funeral Services and Resources	190
殡礼和资源	191

MORNING AND EVENING PRAYER FIRST ORDER

INTRODUCTION

1. The Sentence of the Day or one of the following may be read.

You are worthy, our Lord and God, to receive glory and honour and power, for you created all things, and by your will they existed and were created.

Revelation 4.11

God is spirit, and those who worship him must worship in spirit and truth.

John 4.24

2. A hymn may be sung.

3. The minister reads one or more of these, or other suitable sentences of Scripture.

Hide your face from my sins, and blot out all my iniquities.

Psalm 51.9

Return to the Lord your God, for he is gracious and merciful, slow to anger, and abounding in steadfast love.

Joel 2.13

To the Lord our God belong mercy and forgiveness, for we have rebelled against him, and have not obeyed the voice of the Lord our God by following his laws, which he set before us by his servants the prophets.

Daniel 9.9–10

The Kingdom of God is at hand: repent, and believe in the gospel.

Mark 1.15

I will go to my father, and say to him, 'Father, I have sinned against heaven and before you; I am no longer worthy to be called your son.'

Luke 15.18–19

早祷和晚祷
崇拜程序一

序言

1. 宣召（宣读当日宣召经文，或以下其中一段）

   我们的主，我们的上帝，你配得荣耀、尊贵、权柄，因为你创造了万物，万物因你的旨意被创造而存在。（启4:11）
   上帝是灵，所以敬拜他的必须用心灵和诚实敬拜他。（约4:24）

2. 诗歌

3. 宣读：（主礼宣读一段或更多下列，或其他合适的经文）

   求你转脸不看我的罪，涂去我一切的罪孽。（诗51:9）
   归向耶和华你们的上帝，因为他有恩惠，有怜悯，不轻易发怒，有丰盛的慈爱。（珥2:13）
   主我们的上帝是怜悯饶恕人的，我们却违背了他，没有听从耶和华我们上帝的话，没有遵行他藉僕人众先知向我们颁佈的律法。（但9:9-10）
   日期满了，上帝的国近了。你们要悔改，信福音！（可1:15）
   我要起来，到我父亲那里去，对他说：父亲！我得罪了天，又得罪了你，从今以后，我不配称为你的儿子。（路15:18-19）

If we say that we have no sin, we deceive ourselves, and the truth is not in us. If we confess our sins, he who is faithful and just will forgive us our sins and cleanse us from all unrighteousness.

1 John 1.8–9

4. The minister continues

Dear friends, the Scriptures urge us to acknowledge our sins, and not to conceal them from God our heavenly Father, but to confess them with a penitent and obedient heart, so that we may be forgiven through his infinite goodness and mercy.

We ought always to admit our sins before God, and especially when we come together to give thanks for the good things we have received at his hands, to offer the praise that is his due, to hear his holy word, and to ask what is necessary for the body as well as the soul.

Therefore, let us draw near to the throne of our gracious God, as we pray:

5. All kneel for a general Confession.

Almighty and most merciful Father,
we have strayed from your ways like lost sheep,
we have followed too much
the devices and desires of our own hearts,
we have offended against your holy laws.
We have left undone what we ought to have done,
and we have done what we ought not to have done.
Yet, good Lord, have mercy on us;
restore those who are penitent,
according to your promises declared
in Jesus Christ our Lord.
Grant, most merciful Father, for his sake,
that we may live godly, righteous and sober lives
to the glory of your holy name. Amen.

我们若说自己没有罪，就是欺骗自己，真理就不在我们里面了。我们若认自己的罪，上帝是信实的，是公义的，必要赦免我们的罪，洗淨我们一切的不义。(约壹1:8-9)

4. 主礼

亲爱的朋友们，圣经敦促我们承认自己的罪，不要向上帝隐藏，却要谦卑和顺服的心向上帝忏悔，以致可以因着他无限的良善和怜悯，而饶恕我们的过犯。

我们要常常在上帝面前承认自己的罪，特别是在我们相聚一起感谢上帝丰盛的供应、献上他应得的赞美、聆听他的话语、和祈求他供应我们身体和心灵需要的时候。

因此，让我们来到慈悲上帝的宝座前，一同祷告：

5. 认罪文（会众可跪下）

全能和仁慈的父上帝，
我们像迷失的羊群一样，离开你的道路。
我们常常跟随自己的私慾，触犯你的圣律法。
我们应做的不做，不应做的反去做。
求天父怜悯我们，在我们主耶稣基督里赦免那些愿意悔改的人；
又施恩，使我们能活出圣洁、公义和自律的生命，来荣耀你的圣名。
阿们！

6. The priest stands to pronounce the Absolution.

The God and Father of our Lord Jesus Christ has no pleasure in the death of sinners, but would rather they should turn from their wickedness and live.

He has given authority to his ministers to declare to his people who repent the forgiveness of sins.

God pardons all who truly repent and believe his holy gospel.

And so we ask him to grant us true repentance, and his holy Spirit, that what we do now may please him, and that the rest of our lives may be pure and holy; so that at the last we may come to his eternal joy; through Jesus Christ our Lord. **Amen.**

Or, the minister may read one of these sentences of Scripture.

If anyone sins, we have an advocate with the Father, Jesus Christ the righteous. He is the perfect offering for our sins, and not for ours only, but also for the sins of the whole world.

1 John 2.1–2

In this is love, not that we loved God,
but that he loved us and sent his Son
to be the perfect offering for our sins.

1 John 4.10

7. Except on Sundays, when the Introduction is used the service may begin here.

Open our lips, O Lord;
   and we shall declare your praise.
O God, make speed to save us.
   O Lord, make haste to help us.

All stand.

Glory to God; Father, Son, and Holy Spirit:
   as in the beginning, so now, and for ever. Amen.
Let us praise the Lord.
   The Lord's name be praised.

Morning Prayer continues on page 8.

Evening Prayer continues on page 14.

6. 牧师（站立宣读赦罪文）

上帝不愿罪人沉沦死亡，却愿罪人从罪恶中回转。

他赐给他仆人权柄，向愿意悔改的人宣告赦免。

上帝拯救所有愿意真心悔改，并相信福音的人。求他赐下圣灵，和真正悔改的心给我们，使我们能讨他喜悦，并在我们余下的生命中活出圣洁，以致能进他永恒的喜乐中。奉我们主耶稣基督的名祷告。阿们！

（或读以下其中一段经文）

若有人犯罪，在父那里我们有一位中保，就是那义者耶稣基督。他为我们的罪作了赎罪祭，不单是为我们的罪，也是为普天下人的罪。(约壹2:1-2)

不是我们爱上帝，而是上帝爱我们，差他的儿子为我们的罪作了赎罪祭；这就是爱。(约壹4:10)

7. （除主日外，崇拜可以由此开始）

主啊，求你使我们的口唇张开；
　（会众）我们的口便传扬赞美你的话。
上帝啊，请你快快拯救我们；
　（会众）请快快帮助我们。

全体起立

荣耀归於上帝，圣父、圣子、圣灵：
　（会众）起初这样，现在这样，以後也这样，直到永远。阿们！
让我们赞美主
　（会众）主的名配得称颂

早祷请继续第 9 页

晚祷转到第 15 页

7

AT MORNING PRAYER

8. Psalm 95 (Venite)

O come, let us sing out to the Lord:
>   let us shout in triumph to the rock of our salvation.

Let us come before his face with thanksgiving:
>   and cry out to him joyfully in psalms.

For the Lord is a great God:
>   and a great king above all gods.

In his hand are the depths of the earth:
>   and the peaks of the mountains are his also.

The sea is his and he made it:
>   his hands moulded dry land.

Come, let us worship and bow down:
>   and kneel before the Lord our maker.

For he is the Lord our God:
>   we are his people and the sheep of his pasture.

Today if only you would hear his voice:
>   'Do not harden your hearts as Israel did in the wilderness;

'When your forebears tested me:
>   put me to proof though they had seen my works.

'Forty years long I loathed that generation and said:
>   "It is a people who err in their hearts,

for they do not know my ways";
>   'Of whom I swore in my wrath:

"They shall not enter my rest."'
>   Glory to God; Father, Son and Holy Spirit:

as in the beginning, so now, and for ever. Amen.

Or, In Eastertide, the Hymn to the Risen Christ

早祷

8. 诗篇95（赞美诗）

1 来啊，我们要向耶和华歌唱，
　　向拯救我们的磐石欢呼！
2 我们要以感谢来到他面前，
　　用诗歌向他欢呼！
3 因耶和华是伟大的上帝，
　　是超越万上帝的大君王。
4 地的深处在他手中；
　　山的高峰也属他。
5 海洋属他，是他造的；
　　旱地也是他手造成的。
6 来啊，我们要俯伏敬拜，
　　在造我们的耶和华面前跪拜。
7 因为他是我们的上帝；
　　我们是他草场的百姓，是他手中的羊。
　　惟愿你们今天听他的话！
8 你们不可硬着心，像在米利巴，
　　就是在旷野玛撒的日子。
9 那时，你们的祖宗试我，探我，
　　并且观看我的作为。
10 四十年之久，我厌烦那世代，说：
　　「这是心里迷糊的百姓，
　　竟不知道我的道路！」
11 所以，我在怒中起誓：
　　「他们断不可进入我的安息！」

荣耀归于上帝，圣父、圣子、圣灵：
起初这样，现在这样，以后也这样，直到永远。阿们！

复活期，可加入有关基督昇天的诗歌

9. The Psalm(s) of the day

After the last psalm

Glory to God; Father, Son and Holy Spirit:
  as in the beginning, so now, and for ever. Amen.

10. The first Reading, from the Old Testament, is announced by the name of the book, the number of the chapter, and 'beginning at verse…'

After the reading, the reader says 'Here ends the first reading'.

11. The Song of the Church (Te Deum) or a similar hymn of praise

We praise you, O God:
  we acclaim you as the Lord.
All creation worships you:
  the Father everlasting.
To you all angels, all the powers of heaven:
  the cherubim and seraphim, sing in endless praise:
Holy, holy, holy Lord, God of power and might:
  heaven and earth are full of your glory.
The glorious company of apostles praise you:
  The noble fellowship of prophets praise you.
The white-robed army of martyrs praise you:
  Throughout the world, the holy Church acclaims you:

9. 颂读诗篇（经课表）

（颂读诗篇後，会众一同回应）

　　荣耀归於上帝，圣父、圣子、圣灵；
　　起初这样，现在这样，以後也这样，直到永远。阿们！

10. 颂读旧约（经课表）
　'第一段宣读经文，记载在旧约_____，第_____章，第_____节，…。'

宣读完毕，宣读者说：'第一段经文宣读完毕。'

11. 赞美颂 或诗歌

Father, of majesty unbounded:

> your true and only Son, worthy of all praise,
>
> and the Holy Spirit, advocate and guide.

You, Lord Christ, are the King of glory:

> the eternal Son of the Father.

When you took our flesh to set us free:

> you humbly chose the Virgin's womb.

You overcame the sting of death:

> and opened the kingdom of heaven to all believers.

You are seated at God's right hand in glory:

> We believe that you will come to be our judge.

Come then, Lord, and help your people,
bought with the price of your own blood:

> and bring us with your saints to glory everlasting.

The Song may end here, or continue

> Save your people, Lord, and bless your inheritance:
>
> > Govern and uphold them now and always.
>
> Day by day we bless you:
>
> > We praise your name for ever.
>
> Keep us today, Lord, from all sin:
>
> > Have mercy on us, Lord, have mercy.
>
> Lord, show us your love and mercy:
>
> > for we have put our trust in you.
>
> In you, Lord, is our hope:
>
> > let us never be put to shame.

12. The second Reading, from the New Testament
After the reading, the reader says 'Here ends the second reading'.

Morning Prayer continues on page 16.

12. 颂读新约（经课表）

宣读完毕，宣读者说：'第二段经文宣读完毕。'

早祷请转第 17页

AT EVENING PRAYER

9a. The Psalm(s) of the day
After the last psalm

> Glory to God; Father, Son and Holy Spirit:
> as in the beginning, so now, and for ever. Amen.

10a. The first Reading, from the Old Testament, is announced by the name of the book, the number of the chapter, and 'beginning at verse…'
After the reading, the reader says 'Here ends the first reading'.

11a. The Song of Mary (Magnificat) or a similar hymn

> My soul proclaims the greatness of the Lord:
> > my spirit rejoices in God my Saviour,
>
> Who has looked with favour on his lowly servant:
> > from this day all generations will call me blessed;
>
> The Almighty has done great things for me:
> > and holy is his name.
>
> God has mercy on those who fear him:
> > from generation to generation.
>
> The Lord has shown strength with his arm:
> > and scattered the proud in their conceit,
>
> Casting down the mighty from their thrones:
> > and lifting up the lowly.
>
> God has filled the hungry with good things:
> > and sent the rich away empty.
>
> He has come to the aid of his servant Israel:
> > to remember the promise of mercy,
>
> The promise made to our forebears:
> > to Abraham and his children for ever.
>
> Glory to God; Father, Son, and Holy Spirit;
> > as in the beginning, so now, and for ever. Amen.

12a. The second Reading, from the New Testament
After the reading, the reader says 'Here ends the second reading'.
The service continues on page 18.

晚祷

9a. 颂读诗篇（经课表）
（颂读诗篇後，会众一同回应）

荣耀归於上帝，圣父、圣子、圣灵；
起初这样，现在这样，以後也这样，直到永远。阿们！

10a. 颂读旧约（经课表）
'第一段宣读经文，记载在旧约_____，第_____章，第_____节，…。'
宣读完毕，宣读者说：'第一段经文宣读完毕。'

11a. 诗歌

我心尊主为大：
　我灵以神我的救主为乐，
因为他顾念他使女的卑微：
　从今以后，万代要称我有福；
那有权能的为我成就了大事：
　他的名为圣.
他怜悯敬畏他的人：
　直到世世代代.
他用膀臂施展大能：
　狂傲的人正心里妄想就被他赶散了.
他叫有权柄的失位：
　叫卑贱的升高；
叫饥饿的得饱美食：
　叫富足的空手回去.
他扶助了他的仆人以色列：
为要记念亚伯拉罕和他的后裔，
施怜悯直到永远：
正如从前对我们列祖所说的话."

12a. 颂读新约（经课表）
宣读完毕，宣读者说：'第二段经文宣读完毕。'
请转第 19页继续崇拜

AT MORNING PRAYER

13. The Song of Zechariah (Benedictus) or a similar hymn

Blessed be the Lord, the God of Israel:
> who has come to his people and set them free.

The Lord has raised up for us a mighty Saviour:
> born of the house of his servant David.

Through the holy prophets, God promised of old:
> to save us from our enemies, from the hands of all who hate us,

To show mercy to our forebears:
and to remember his holy covenant.

> This was the oath God swore to our father Abraham:

to set us free from the hands of our enemies,
> Free to worship him without fear:

holy and righteous before him, all the days of our life.

> And you, child, shall be called the prophet of the Most High:

for you will go before the Lord to prepare his way,
> To give his people knowledge of salvation:

by the forgiveness of their sins.

> In the tender compassion of our God:

the dawn from on high shall break upon us,
> To shine on those who dwell in darkness and

the shadow of death:
> and to guide our feet into the way of peace.

Glory to God; Father, Son, and Holy Spirit:
> as in the beginning, so now, and for ever. Amen.

The service continues on page 20.

早祷

13. 撒迦利亚的颂歌，或其他诗歌

「主 --- 以色列的上帝是應當稱頌的！
因他眷顧他的百姓，為他們施行救贖，
在他僕人大衛家中，
為我們興起了拯救的角，
正如主藉著古時候聖先知的口所說的，
『他拯救我們脫離仇敵，
脫離一切恨我們之人的手。
他向我們列祖施憐憫，
記得他的聖約，
就是他對我們祖宗亞伯拉罕所起的誓，
叫我們既從仇敵手中被救出來，
就可以終身在他面前，
無所懼怕地用聖潔和公義事奉他。
孩子啊，你要稱為至高者的先知；
因為你要走在主的前面，為他預備道路，
叫他的百姓因罪得赦，
認識救恩；
因我們上帝憐憫的心腸，
叫清晨的日光從高天臨到我們，
要照亮坐在黑暗中死蔭裏的人，
把我們的腳引到和平的路上。』」

荣耀归於上帝，圣父、圣子、圣灵；
起初这样，现在这样，以後也这样，直到永远。阿们！

请转第 21 页继续崇拜

AT EVENING PRAYER

13a. The Song of Simeon (Nunc Dimittis) or a similar hymn

Now, Lord, you let your servant go in peace:
   your word has been fulfilled.
My own eyes have seen the salvation:
   which you have prepared in the sight of every people:
A light to reveal you to the nations:
   and the glory of your people Israel.
Glory to God; Father, Son, and Holy Spirit:
   as in the beginning, so now, and for ever. Amen.

The service continues on page 20.

晚祷

13a. 西面的颂歌，或其他诗歌

「主啊，如今可以照你的話，
容你的僕人安然去世；
因為我的眼睛已經看見你的救恩，
就是你在萬民面前所預備的：
是啟示外邦人的光，
是你民以色列的榮耀。」

荣耀归於上帝，圣父、圣子、圣灵；
起初这样，现在这样，以後也这样，直到永远。阿们！

请转第 21 页继续崇拜

14. The Apostles' Creed

> I believe in God, the Father almighty,
>> creator of heaven and earth.
>
> I believe in Jesus Christ, God's only Son, our Lord,
>> who was conceived by the Holy Spirit,
>>
>> born of the virgin Mary,
>>
>> suffered under Pontius Pilate,
>>
>> was crucified, died, and was buried;
>>
>> he descended to the dead.
>>
>> On the third day he rose from the dead;
>>
>> he ascended into heaven,
>>
>> and is seated at the right hand of the Father;
>>
>> from there he will come to judge
>>
>> the living and the dead.
>
> I believe in the Holy Spirit,
>> the holy catholic Church,
>>
>> the communion of saints,
>>
>> the forgiveness of sins,
>>
>> the resurrection of the body,
>>
>> and the life everlasting. Amen.

15. The Prayers

> The Lord be with you.
>> **And also with you.**
>
> Let us pray.

All kneel.

16. **The Litany may replace these prayers when appropriate.**

> Lord, have mercy on us.
>> **Christ, have mercy on us.**
>
> Lord, have mercy on us.

14. 使徒信经

我相信上帝，全能的父，创造天地的主。
我相信我们的主耶稣基督，上帝的独生子，
因圣灵感孕，由童贞女玛利亚所生，
在本丢彼拉多手下受难，受死，埋葬，降在阴间，
第三天从死人中复活，升天，坐在全能父上帝的右边，
他将再临审判活人死人。

我相信圣灵，
圣而公之教会，
我信圣徒相通，
我信罪得赦免，
我信身体复活，
我信永生。

阿们！

15. 祷告

愿主与你们同在。
也与你同在。
我们一同祷告。

会众跪下或坐下

16. 可用其他祷文代替以下祷文

求主怜悯我们。
求基督怜悯我们。
求主怜悯我们。

Our Father in heaven,
**hallowed be your name,
your kingdom come,
your will be done,
on earth as in heaven.**
Give us today our daily bread.
Forgive us our sins
as we forgive those who sin against us.
Save us from the time of trial
and deliver us from evil.
For the kingdom, the power, and the glory are yours
now and for ever. Amen.
Lord, show us your mercy,
and grant us your salvation.
Keep our nation under your care,
and guide us in justice and truth.
Clothe your ministers with righteousness,
and make your chosen people joyful.
Lord, save your people,
and bless your inheritance.
Give peace in our time, O Lord,
for you are our help and strength.
Create in us clean hearts, O God,
and renew us by your Holy Spirit.

17. The Collect of the Day

18. The Collect for Peace

O God, the author and lover of peace, in knowledge of whom stands our eternal life, whose service is perfect freedom; defend your servants in all assaults of our enemies, that, surely trusting in your defence, we may not fear the power of any adversaries, through the might of Jesus Christ our Lord. **Amen.**

我们在天上的父，愿人都尊你的名为圣。
愿你的国降临。愿你的旨意行在地上，
如同行在天上。我们日用的饮食，今日赐给我们。
饶恕我们的罪，如同我们饶恕得罪我们的人。
不叫我们遇见试探，救我们脱离凶恶。
因为国度、权柄、荣耀，全是你的，
直到永远，阿们。

求主向我们发慈悲，
求主赐恩拯救我们。
求主保守我们的国家，
求主带领我们在公义和真理中。
愿主的仆人都披上公义，
愿主的选民得享欢乐。
求主拯救你的百姓，
求主赐福你的产业。
求主使我们得享平安，
因为你是我们的帮助和力量。
求主为我们造清洁的心，
求圣灵更新我们。

17. 本日祝文（可参考英文版公祷书）

18. 求安祝文

上帝是平安的根源，并喜悦人和睦，
认识主就是永生，事奉主就是自由。
求主在仇敌攻击我们的时候，保护你的仆人，
使我们专心倚靠主的保护，不怕敌人的势力。
这都是靠着我们主耶稣基督。**阿们！**

19. **Morning Collect**

Lord, our heavenly Father, almighty and everlasting God, we thank you for bringing us safely to this day: keep us by your mighty power, and grant that we fall into no sin, neither run into any kind of danger; but lead and govern us in all things, that we may always do what is righteous in your sight; through Jesus Christ our Lord. **Amen.**

or, Evening Collect

Lighten our darkness, Lord, we pray: and in your great mercy defend us from all perils and dangers of this night; for the love of your only Son our Saviour Jesus Christ. **Amen.**

20. **An anthem or hymn may be sung.**

21. **Prayers are offered for those in authority, for the Church and for all people. The following, or other appropriate prayers, may be used.**

A Prayer for all in Authority
Almighty God, fountain of all goodness,
we humbly pray you to bless our sovereign lady,
Queen Elizabeth, and all who govern us:
may all things be ordered in wisdom,
righteousness, and peace,
to the honour of your holy name,
and the good of your Church and people;
through Jesus Christ our Lord. **Amen.**

Or

Lord God almighty, ruler of the nations of the earth,
give wisdom to the Prime Minister of Australia (N)
[and the Premier of this State (N)],
to the members of Parliament (especially N)
and to all who hold office in this land.
Grant that their decisions may be based on wise counsel,
so that peace and welfare,
truth and justice may prevail among us,
and make us a blessing to other nations; u
through Jesus Christ our Lord. **Amen.**

19. 早祷祝文

全能永生的父，感谢你带领我们，平安到了今天。求主保守我们，不陷在罪中，不遇见危险，引导我们常行主所喜悦的事。这都是靠着我们主耶稣基督。阿们！

或晚祷祝文

求主光照我们的黑暗，怜悯我们，保守我们今夜不遇危险；因着你的爱子，救主耶稣基督，应允我们。阿们！

20. 诗歌

21. 为掌权者、教会和所有人祷告

可用以下，或其他的祷文

为掌权者祷告
全能的上帝，良善的泉源，我们谦卑向你祷告：
求你赐福我们的女王伊利沙伯，和其他掌权者。愿一切的管治，都充满智慧、公义和平安，使你的名得荣耀；并有益於你的教会和百姓，奉我们主耶稣基督的名求。**阿们！**

或

全能的上帝，统治万邦的主：
求你赐智慧给我们澳洲总理（姓名），本省的省长（姓名），国会的议员们，和所有管理这国家的官员。使他们能作出明智的决策，让我们可以生活在平安、幸福、真理和公义中。
也使我们成为其他国家的祝福。奉我们主耶稣基督的名求。**阿们！**

A Prayer for the Church

Almighty and eternal God, you alone work great marvels:

send down your Spirit of saving grace on all Christian people.

Bless our bishops, clergy and congregations:

pour upon them the continual dew of your blessing

that they may truly please you.

Grant this, for the honour of Jesus Christ

our advocate and mediator. Amen.

A Prayer for all People

God of providence, God of love, we pray for all people: make your way known to them, your saving power among all nations.

We pray for the welfare of your Church throughout the world: guide and govern it by your Spirit, so that all who call themselves Christians may be led in the way of truth and hold the faith in unity of spirit, in the bond of peace, and in righteousness of life.

We commend to your fatherly goodness all who are afflicted or distressed in body, mind or circumstances (especially...). Relieve them according to their needs, giving them patience in their sufferings, and deliverance from their afflictions. This we ask for the sake of Jesus Christ our Saviour. Amen.

A concluding prayer from the Liturgy of St John Chrysostom

Lord, you have given us grace to agree in these our prayers, and you have promised that when two or three ask together in your name you will grant their requests. Fulfil now, Lord, our desires and prayers as may be best for us. Grant us, in this life, knowledge of your truth and in the age to come, life eternal. Amen.

为教会祷告

全能永生的上帝,你手作奇妙大工:
求你赐给信徒恩典的灵。祝福我们的主教们、牧者们和会众。让你的恩典不断倾倒在他们身上,使他们可以讨你喜悦。因我们的中保耶稣基督荣耀的名,应允我们。**阿们!**

为世人祷告

慈爱的上帝,我们为全地的人向你祷告:求你使人们能认识你,使你的权能充满全地。

我们为普世的教会祷告:求你的灵引导和管理教会,使凡称为基督徒的,都蒙指引,归入真道,同心坚守信仰,彼此和睦,活出公义。

我们把身体软弱,心灵忧伤,和身处困境的人,都交托给慈悲的天父。求主安慰、医治他们,在困苦中给他们有忍耐的心,拯救他们脱离困苦。奉我们救主耶稣基督的名求。**阿们!**

总结祷文(圣屈梭多模祷文)

求主赐恩典给我们,叫我们在这时候同心祷告;你曾应许我们,若有两三个人奉你的名聚集祷告,你必在他们中间。现在我们所愿所求的,若是与我们有益,求主应允;叫我们今世明白主的真道,来世得享永生。**阿们!**

A general thanksgiving

Almighty God and merciful Father,
we give you hearty thanks
for all your goodness and loving-kindness to us
and to all people.
We bless you for our creation and preservation,
and all the blessings of this life;
but above all, for your immeasurable love
in the redemption of the world by our Lord Jesus Christ,
for the means of grace, and for the hope of glory.
And, we pray, give us such a sense of all your mercies,
that our hearts may be truly thankful
and that we may praise you
not only with our lips, but in our lives,
serving you in holiness and righteousness all our days,
through Jesus Christ, our Lord,
to whom with you and the Holy Spirit,
be honour and glory, now and for ever. **Amen**
The grace of the Lord Jesus Christ,
and the love of God,
and the fellowship of the Holy Spirit,
be with us all evermore. Amen.

总谢文

全能的上帝，慈悲的父神，
我们谦卑感谢主，
因为你赐恩惠、仁慈予我们，也赐给万人。
我们感谢你创造我们，保护我们，
并将今世各样的福，赐给我们；
更感谢主无穷的慈爱，
藉着我们的救赎主耶稣基督，
赐给我们救赎的恩典，和荣耀的盼望。
求主使我们常常思念你一切的恩惠，诚心感谢赞美你。
又叫我们不但口里颂扬你，
也在生活中彰显出来，将自己献给你，
终身在你面前，用圣洁、公义侍奉你。
这都是靠着我们主耶稣基督，
但愿尊贵、荣耀，归与圣父、圣子、圣灵，
直到永远。**阿们！**

**愿主耶稣基督的恩惠、上帝的慈爱、圣灵的感动，常与我们众人同在！
阿们！**

MORNING AND EVENING PRAYER SECOND ORDER

GATHERING IN GOD'S NAME

1. The minister reads one or more of these or other suitable sentences of Scripture.

Through Christ let us offer up a sacrifice of praise to God,
the fruit of lips that acknowledge his name.

Hebrews 13.15

Worthy is the Lamb who was slain,
to receive power and wealth and wisdom and strength
and honour and glory and praise!

Revelation 5.12

Holy, holy, holy is the Lord of hosts,
who was, and is, and is to come!

Revelation 4.8

Blessed be the God and Father of our Lord Jesus Christ!
By his great mercy we have been born anew
to a living hope
through the resurrection of Jesus Christ from the dead.

1 Peter 1.3

2. These or similar responses are used.

Open our lips, O Lord,
  and we shall declare your praise.
This is the day that the Lord has made,
  we will rejoice and be glad in it.

In the Easter season may be added

Christ is risen!
  He is risen indeed.

3. Hymn(s) of praise and/or invocation may be sung.

早祷和晚祷
崇拜程序二
序言

1. 宣读：（主礼宣读一段或更多下列，或其他合适的经文）

    我们应当靠著耶稣，常常以颂讚为祭献给上帝，这就是那承认主名之人嘴唇所结的果子。（来13:15）

    被杀的羔羊配得
    权能、丰富、智慧、力量、
    尊贵、荣耀、颂讚。（启5:12）

    圣哉！圣哉！圣哉！
    主—全能的上帝；
    昔在、今在、以后永在！（启4:8）

    愿颂讚归于我们主耶稣基督的父上帝！他曾照自己的大怜悯，藉着耶稣基督从死里复活，重生了我们，叫我们有活泼的盼望。

2. 回应

    主啊，求你使我们的口唇张开；
    （会众）我们的口便传扬赞美你的话。
    这是耶和华所定的日子；
    （会众）我们要欢喜快乐。

复活节加以下回应

    基督已经复活！
    他确实复活了。

3. 诗歌

4. The minister continues in these or similar words.

Friends in Christ,
    we come together to meet with God,
    and to take our part in the building up of his Church.
We will lift up our hearts in thanks and praise,
    hear from God's holy word,
    and pray for this world, and for ourselves.
    [Today ...]
The Bible tells us to approach God confidently,
    through our Lord Jesus Christ.
As we do so, we must confess our sins,
seeking forgiveness through God's boundless
    goodness and mercy.

5. One or more of these or other suitable sentences of Scripture may be read.

God now commands all people everywhere to repent, for he has set a day when he will judge the world with justice by the man he has appointed, Jesus Christ the Lord.

Acts 17.30–31

I will arise and go to my father, and will say to him,
'Father, I have sinned against heaven and before you;
I am no more worthy to be called your son'.

Luke 15.18–19

To the Lord our God belong mercy and forgiveness,
though we have rebelled against him,
and have not obeyed the voice of the Lord our God
by following his laws which he set before us.

Daniel 9.9–10

If we say that we have no sin, we deceive ourselves,
and the truth is not in us.
But if we confess our sins, God is faithful and just,
and will forgive our sins
and cleanse us from all unrighteousness.

1 John 1.8–9

6. Silence may be kept.

4. 主礼

   弟兄姐妹们：
   我们一同与上帝相聚，并尽力建造他的教会。
   我们以感恩和赞美的心仰望主，聆听上帝的圣言，
   并为这世界和我们自己祷告：

   （今天……）

   圣经告诉我们，藉着我们主耶稣基督，可以坦然无惧的来到上帝的面前。因此，我们必须承认我们的罪过，恳求慈悲的上帝赦免我们。

5. 宣读：（主礼宣读一段或更多下列，或其他合适的经文）

   世人蒙昧无知的时候，上帝并不追究，如今却吩咐各处的人都要悔改。　因为他已经定了日子，要藉着他所设立的人按公义审判天下，就是主耶稣基督。（徒17:30-31）
   我要起来，到我父亲那里去，对他说：父亲！我得罪了天，又得罪了你，从今以后，我不配称为你的儿子。（路15:18-19）
   主 - 我们的上帝是怜悯饶恕人的，我们却违背了他，　没有听从耶和华 - 我们上帝的话，没有遵行他藉僕人众先知向我们颁佈的律法。（但9:9-10）

我们若说自己没有罪，就是欺骗自己，真理就不在我们里面了。　我们若认自己的罪，上帝是信实的，是公义的，必要赦免我们的罪，洗淨我们一切的不义。（约壹1:8-9）

6. 片刻安静

The minister continues

So let us draw near to God with sincerity and confidence, and pray together,

God of all mercy,

we humbly admit that we need your help.

We have wandered from your way.

We have sinned in thought, word and deed,

and have failed to do what is right.

You alone can save us.

Have mercy on us,

wipe out our sins and teach us to forgive others.

Bring forth in us the fruit of your Spirit

   that we may live the new life to your glory.

This we ask in the name of Jesus our Saviour. Amen.

7. The minister stands and declares God's forgiveness.

God desires that none should perish,

but that all should turn to Christ, and live.

In response to his call we acknowledge our sins.

God pardons those who humbly repent, and truly believe

   the gospel.

Therefore we have peace with God, through Jesus Christ. **Amen.**

And/or, the minister may read one of these sentences of Scripture.

If anyone sins, we have an advocate with the Father, Jesus Christ the righteous. He is the perfect offering for our sins, and not for ours only, but also for the sins of the whole world.

1 John 2.1–2

In this is love, not that we loved God,

but that he loved us and sent his Son

to be the perfect offering for our sins.

1 John 4.10

主礼继续

让我们一同以真诚和信心来到上帝的面前，一同祷告：
慈悲的上帝：
我们谦卑承认需要你的帮助。我们常常偏行己路。
在思想、言语和行为上得罪了你，应做的没有做。
你是我们唯一的拯救，
求主怜悯我们，抹去我们的过犯，
并教导我们原谅其他人。
赐给我们圣灵的果子，使我们能活出新的生命来荣耀你。
这是奉靠我们救主耶稣基督的名求。
阿们！

7. 赦罪文

上帝不愿一人沉沦，乃愿所有人都转向基督而得生命。要回应上帝的呼召，我们必须承认自己的罪。

上帝赦免所有真心悔改，并相信福音的人。因此，我们可以藉着耶稣基督，与上帝和好。**阿们！**

或/和

主礼可读以下其中一段经文

若有人犯罪，在父那里我们有一位中保，就是那义者耶稣基督。 他为我们的罪作了赎罪祭，不单是为我们的罪，也是为普天下人的罪。（约壹2:1-2）

不是我们爱上帝，而是上帝爱我们，差他的儿子为我们的罪作了赎罪祭；这就是爱。（约壹4:10）

Neither death, nor life, nor angels, nor rulers,
nor things present, nor things to come,
nor powers, nor height, nor depth,
nor anything in all creation,
will be able to separate us from the love of God
in Christ Jesus our Lord.

Romans 8.38–39

8. **All stand. The minister says**

    Give thanks to the Lord, for he is good.
    His steadfast love endures for ever!

The minister greets the people, who may greet one another.

   Grace and peace be with you
   and also with you.

9. **A hymn or song of praise and thanksgiving follows, or one of the following forms may be used.**

    Come, let us sing to the Lord,
    shout to the rock of our salvation.
    Serve the Lord with gladness,
    come before his face with songs of joy.

Or, in the evening

   Come bless the Lord, all you servants of the Lord
   you that stand by night in the house of the Lord.
   Lift up your hands towards the holy place
   and bless the Lord, who made heaven and earth.

无论是死，是活，是天使，是掌权的，
是有权能的，是现在的事，是将来的事，
是高处的，是深处的，是别的受造之物，
都不能使我们与上帝的爱隔绝，
这爱是在我们的主基督耶稣里的。（罗8:38-39）

8. 全体起立

  感谢主，因为他是美善。
  他的慈爱永远长存！

主礼向会众问安，然後会众互相问安

  愿主的恩惠和平安与你们同在。
  也与你同在。

9. 诗歌或以下礼文

  来啊，我们要向耶和华歌唱，
   向拯救我们的磐石欢呼！
  当乐意事奉耶和华，
   当欢唱来到他面前！

或，在晚祷中

  耶和华的众仆人，你们要称颂耶和华，
  夜间站立在耶和华殿中的，你们要称颂耶和华。
  你们当向圣所举手，
  称颂那造天的的耶和华。

THE MINISTRY OF THE WORD

10. The minister offers this prayer, or a suitable alternative, in preparation for the reading and teaching of the Scriptures.

> Heavenly Father,
>   give us wisdom and understanding.
> As we listen to your Word,
>   may we know you better,
>   love you more,
>   and learn to please you in all we do;
> through Jesus Christ our Lord. **Amen.**

The first Reading, from the Old Testament, or as appointed.

The readings may be concluded

> Hear the word of the Lord,
>   **thanks be to God.**

Each reading may be followed by silence, music, meditative response, discussion, dialogue or testimony.

A time of Children's Ministry may be associated with the readings.

11. The Psalm(s) of the day are said or sung here, or may precede the Old Testament reading.

These words may be added after the last psalm

> Glory to God; Father, Son and Holy Spirit:
> as in the beginning, so now, and for ever. Amen.

12. The Canticle, The Song of the Church (page 10, suitable in the morning), The Song of Mary (page 14, suitable in the evening) or other hymn may follow.

圣言职事

10. 主礼用以下，或其他合适的祷文，预备宣读和教导圣经

> 我们在天上的父，求你赐我们智慧和理解力。
> 当我们聆听你话语的时候，
> 让我们能够更认识你，
> 爱你更深，
> 凡事讨你喜悦。
> 奉我们主耶稣基督的名求。**阿们！**

宣读旧约圣经，或其他指定经文

读毕後说：

> 聆听上帝的道。
> **感谢上帝。**
> 每段经文读毕，都可有一段安静、或音乐、或默想、或回应、或讨论、或对话、或见证的时间。
> 儿童事工也可在此时进行。

11. 颂读诗篇（经课表）

读毕後说：

> 荣耀归於上帝，圣父、圣子、圣灵；
> 起初这样，现在这样，直到永远。阿们！

12. 诗歌

13. A Reading or readings from the New Testament.

14. The Canticle, The Song of Zechariah (page 16, suitable in the morning), The Song of Simeon (page 18, suitable in the evening) or other hymn may follow.

15. The Sermon is preached here or later.

16. A time of congregational reflection may follow, involving questions and discussion, and mutual encouragement or warning, based on the sermon and readings.

17. The Apostles' Creed is said or sung. In its place the Song of the Church (Te Deum on page 10) may be used, or another hymn declaring the Christian faith.

>I believe in God, the Father almighty,
>>creator of heaven and earth.
>I believe in Jesus Christ, God's only Son, our Lord,
>>who was conceived by the Holy Spirit,
>>born of the virgin Mary,
>>suffered under Pontius Pilate,
>>was crucified, died, and was buried;
>>he descended to the dead.
>>On the third day he rose from the dead;
>>he ascended into heaven,
>>and is seated at the right hand of the Father;
>>from there he will come to judge
>>the living and the dead.
>I believe in the Holy Spirit,
>>the holy catholic Church,
>>the communion of saints,
>>the forgiveness of sins,
>>the resurrection of the body,
>>and the life everlasting. Amen.

13. 宣读新约

14. 诗歌

15. 讲道

16. 对讲道的回应、讨论、鼓励或忠告

17. 使徒信经

    我相信上帝,全能的父,创造天地的主。

    我相信我们主耶稣基督,上帝的独生子,
    因圣灵感孕,由童贞女玛利亚所生,
    在本丢彼拉多手下受难,受死,埋葬,降在阴间,
    第三天从死人中复活,升天,坐在全能父上帝的右边,
    他将再临审判活人死人。

    我相信圣灵,
    我信圣而公之教会,
    我信圣徒相通,
    我信罪得赦免,
    我信身体复活,
    我信永生。

    阿们!

THE MINISTRY OF PRAYER

18. The minister says

The Lord be with you.
And also with you.
Let us join together in the prayer which Jesus gave us.
Our Father in heaven,
hallowed be your name,
your kingdom come,
your will be done,
on earth as in heaven.
Give us today our daily bread.
Forgive us our sins
as we forgive those who sin against us.
Save us from the time of trial
and deliver us from evil.
For the kingdom, the power, and the glory are yours
now and for ever. Amen.

19. The minister continues

Be exalted, Lord, above the heavens,
let your glory cover the earth.
Keep our nation under your care,
and guide us in justice and truth.
Let your way be known on earth,
your saving power among all nations.
Send out your light and your truth,
that we may tell of your saving works.
Have mercy on the poor and oppressed.
Hear the cry of those in need.
Hear our prayers, O Lord,
for we put our trust in you.

20. The Collect of the Day

祷告

18. 主礼

 愿主与你同在。
 也与你同在。

让我们同读主祷文：

 我们在天上的父，愿人都尊你的名为圣。
 愿你的国降临。愿你的旨意行在地上，
 如同行在天上。我们日用的饮食，今日赐给我们。
 饶恕我们的罪，如同我们饶恕得罪我们的人。
 不叫我们遇见试探，救我们脱离凶恶。
 因为国度、权柄、荣耀，全是你的，
 直到永远，阿们。

19. 主礼

 上帝啊，願你崇高過於諸天，
 願你的榮耀高過全地。
 愿你看顾我们的国家，
 带领我们在公义和真理中。
 讓全地得知你的道路，
 萬國得知你的救恩。
 求你發出你的亮光和信實，
 使我们知道你的救赎大工。
 求你施怜悯给贫穷和被压迫的人。
 聆听有需要者的求告声。
 主啊，垂听我们的祷告，
 我们全心信靠你。

20. 本日祝文（可参考英文版公祷书）

21. The minister may continue

> Let your requests be made known unto God.
> **In everything give thanks.**

Prayers and thanksgivings may be offered

For the whole created order, especially…

For the nations and peoples of the earth…
For those in authority in this land…
For the Church, its leaders and members…
For our community, families and friends…
For those who are in need…
For particular situations…

After each prayer the following or similar responses may be used.

> Father, hear our prayer, Lord, in your mercy,
> **through Jesus Christ our Lord. hear our prayer.**

22. The minister may continue in these or similar words.

> Let any who needs the comfort and strength of God's grace
> come forward for the ministry of the laying on of hands.

The minister may invite those who desire the laying on of hands,
or similar ministry, to come forward to receive

prayer for healing…
supportive prayer for a crisis or special occasion…
encouragement in their own ministries…
affirmation or reaffirmation of faith…
The minister may be assisted by others.
Silence, music or songs may accompany these prayers.

21. 主礼

    愿上帝应允你们的祈求。
    　凡事感恩。

祷告和感恩：

为一切受造之物祷告…

为所有国家和人民祷告…
为本国的掌权者祷告…
为教会、教会领袖和会众祷告…
为我们的群体、家庭、朋友祷告…
为那些有需要的人祷告…
特别为＿＿＿＿祷告…
每一段祷告後，都可有以下的回应：

    求主怜悯，垂听我们的祷告，
    垂听我们的祷告，奉我们主耶稣基督的名求。

22. 主礼（可用以下或类似的方式）

    若你需要得到上帝的安慰或力量，请上前来，我们为你按手祷告。

主礼可邀请希望接受按手祷告的人上前

为医治祷告…
为在困境中，或特殊的事件祷告…
为各人在不同事奉中需要鼓励而祷告…
为确定或重申自己的信仰祷告…
其他同工可帮助主礼或牧者为其他人祷告。
祷告时可以安静、或音乐或诗歌作背景。

23. The prayers conclude with one or both of the following.

> Faithful God,
> you have promised to hear the prayers
> of all who ask in Jesus' name.
> In your mercy, accept our prayers.
> Give us what we have asked in faith,
> according to your will;
> through Jesus Christ our Lord. **Amen.**

From the Liturgy of St John Chrysostom

> Lord, you have given us grace to agree in these our prayers, and you have promised that when two or three ask together in your name you will grant their requests. Fulfil now, Lord, our desires and prayers as may be best for us. Grant us, in this life, knowledge of your truth and in the age to come, life eternal. **Amen.**

THE SENDING OUT OF GOD'S PEOPLE

Hymns or songs may be used at any appropriate point in this section.

24. Notices and other announcements may be made.

25. A collection may be received, accompanied by appropriate Scripture sentences, silence, song, or instrumental music.

The collection may be presented in silence, or the following or another suitable prayer may be used.

> Blessed are you, Lord, God of all creation.
> Through your goodness we have these gifts to share.
> Accept and use our offerings for your glory
> and for the service of your kingdom.
> **Blessed be God for ever.**

26. Corporate acts of commitment and commissioning may take place, with appropriate gestures and prayers.

23. 用以下的一段或两段作结束祷告

> 信实的上帝啊，你承诺若我们奉耶稣的名祷告，你必垂听。
> 愿你按着你的旨意，应允我们的祷告。
> 奉我们主耶稣基督的名求。**阿们！**

或/和 圣屈梭多模祷文

> 求主赐恩典予我们，叫我们在这时候同心祷告；你曾应许我们，若有两三个人奉你的名聚集祷告，你必在他们中间。现在我们所愿所求的，若是与我们有益，求主应允；叫我们今世明白主的真道，来世得享永生。**阿们！**

差遣

可在以下任何合适处加入诗歌

24. 报告

25. 奉献（可用读经、安静、诗歌或音乐配合）

奉献後可以安静，或以下祷文，或其他祷文结束。

> 創造萬有的主上帝，我們讚美你，你滿有恩慈，將各種恩典賜給我們。求你悦纳我们的奉献，使用在你国度的事工，来荣耀你的名。
> **愿赞美永远归於上帝。**

26. 各种差派、送别或交办事务等礼仪可在此时进行

27. One of the following, or a similar prayer, is said.

> Eternal God and Father,
> **by whose power we are created,**
> **and by whose love we are redeemed:**
> **Guide and strengthen us by your Spirit,**
> **that we may give ourselves to your service,**
> **and live this day in love to one another**
> **and to you;**
> **through Jesus Christ our Lord. Amen.**

Or

> Lord Jesus Christ,
> **send us out with confidence in your word**
> **to tell the world of your saving acts,**
> **and bring glory to your name. Amen.**

28. The minister says one of the following

> The grace of the Lord Jesus Christ, and the love of God,
> and the fellowship of the Holy Spirit,
> be with us all. **Amen**.

Or

> May the Lord bless you and keep you;
> May the Lord make his face to shine upon you,
> and be gracious to you.
> May the Lord lift up his countenance upon you,
> and give you peace. **Amen**.

29. The minister says

> Go in peace to love and serve the Lord:
> **In the name of Christ. Amen.**

27. 以下一段，或类似的祷文

　　永生的上帝，天父：
　　你用大能创造了我们，
　　以慈爱救赎了我们。
　　求你的圣灵赐力量和引导我们，使我们能尽心服侍你，
　　并活出爱上帝和爱人的生命。
　　奉我们主耶稣基督的名求。阿们！

或

　　主耶稣基督：
　　求你赐给我们对你话语的信心，
　　差遣我们出去，向世界宣告你的救赎大工，
　　使荣耀都归於你的名。阿们！

28. 主礼

　　愿主耶稣基督的恩惠、上帝的慈爱、圣灵的感动，常与我们众人同在！
　　阿们！

或

　　願耶和華賜福給你，保護你。
　　願耶和華使他的臉光照你，賜恩給你。
　　願耶和華向你仰臉，賜你平安。**阿们！**

29. 主礼

　　你们要平平安安的去敬爱主，服侍主：
　　奉基督的名。阿们！

THE HOLY COMMUNION SECOND ORDER

GATHERING IN GOD'S NAME

1. A psalm, hymn, or anthem may be sung when the ministers enter or after the greeting. A seasonal sentence may be used here or after 3.

2. An Invocation, or an Acclamation such as follows, may be said before or after the greeting.

   Blessed be God: Father, Son and Holy Spirit.
   Blessed be God's kingdom, now and for ever.

In Lent and on other penitential occasions

   Bless the Lord who forgives all our sins,
   whose mercy endures for ever.

3. The Greeting. The priest greets the people in these or other suitable words.

   The grace of the Lord Jesus Christ, and the love of God, and the fellowship of the Holy Spirit, be with you all.
   And also with you.

Or

   The Lord be with you.
   And also with you.

Or, from Easter Day to Pentecost

   Christ is risen. (Alleluia.)
   He is risen indeed. (Alleluia.)

圣餐崇拜
程序二

奉上帝的名聚会

1. 当牧师进入教堂时或问安后唱诗歌,或与节期相关的礼文,或放在*3以后。

2. 主礼选读以下礼文

   赞美圣父,圣子,圣灵三一真神。
   赞美上帝的国直到永远。

在大斋期或其他认罪求告的情形下

   赞美这位赦免我们罪恶的上帝,
   他的慈爱存到永远。

3. 牧师用以下或合适的礼文向众人问安。

   愿主耶稣基督的恩惠,上帝的慈爱,和圣灵的感动交通常与你们同在。

或

   愿主与你们同在, **也与你同在。**

从大斋期到五旬节

   基督已经复活了。哈里路亚。
   他真的复活了。 哈里路亚。

4. This Prayer of Preparation may be said.

> Let us pray.
> **Almighty God,**
> **to whom all hearts are open,**
> **all desires known,**
> **and from whom no secrets are hidden:**
> **cleanse the thoughts of our hearts**
> **by the inspiration of your Holy Spirit,**
> **that we may perfectly love you,**
> **and worthily magnify your holy name,**
> **through Christ our Lord. Amen.**

Prayers 5 to 10 may be used according to local and seasonal custom, in any appropriate form and sequence.

5. The Two Great Commandments, the Ten Commandments, or other suitable passages are said when the confession follows.

> 'Hear, O Israel, the Lord our God, the Lord is one; you shall love the Lord your God with all your heart, and with all your soul, and with all your mind, and with all your strength.' Jesus said: 'This is the great and first commandment. And a second is like it: you shall love your neighbour as yourself.'

4. 洁心祷文 (让我们同心祷告)

    让我们祷告：
    全能的上帝，凡人的心，在主面前无不显明，
    心里所羡慕的，主都知道，
    心里所隐藏的，也瞒不过主。
    求主用圣灵的感化，洁净我们心里的意念，
    使我们尽心爱主，恭敬归荣耀与主的圣名。
    这都是靠着我们的主耶稣基督。
    阿们。

5. 诫命总纲：

"听啊，以色列，我们的上帝是独一的真神，你要尽心，尽性，尽意，尽力爱主你的上帝。" 主耶稣说："这是第一最大诫命，其次爱人如己也是这样。"

6. A deacon or other minister may introduce the Confession with a seasonal introduction or other suitable words.

Silence may be kept.

Let us confess our sins in penitence and faith, confident in God's forgiveness.
**Merciful God,
our maker and our judge,
we have sinned against you
in thought, word, and deed,
and in what we have failed to do:
we have not loved you with our whole heart;
we have not loved our neighbours as ourselves;
we repent, and are sorry for all our sins.
Father, forgive us.
Strengthen us to love and obey you
in newness of life;
through Jesus Christ our Lord. Amen.**

7. The Absolution. Standing, the priest says,

Almighty God,
who has promised forgiveness to all who turn to him in faith:
pardon you and set you free from all your sins,
strengthen you in all goodness
and keep you in eternal life,
through Jesus Christ our Lord. **Amen.**

8. Lord, have mercy (Kyrie eleison)

**Lord, have mercy (Kyrie eleison)
Christ, have mercy (Christe eleison)
Lord, have mercy (Kyrie eleison)**

6. 会吏和其他传道人可按教会年历，或其他合适的祷告文，带领会众认罪。

请静默片刻,同心祷告：

 让我们以谦卑信靠的心，并确信上帝的赦免。
 慈悲的上帝，
 创造和审判我们的主，我们得罪了你。
 我们承认在思想，言语和行为上，
 常常得罪了你；
 应做的不做，不应做的反去做。
 我们没有尽心爱你；
 也没有爱人如己。
 现在我们痛心懊悔，
 恳求你施怜悯，因着圣子我们主耶稣基督，
 饶恕我们的已往，
 扶助我们的现在，
 引导我们的将来；
 好叫我们乐意遵行你的旨意，蒙你悦纳，
 而归荣耀给你的圣名。阿们。

7. 赦罪文。牧师起立说：

 全能的上帝应许，藉着我们主耶稣基督，凭信心来到他面前求赦罪的，必得着赦免，从罪中得释放。主必增强你们行善的力量，保守你们进入永生。**阿门。**

8. '上帝怜悯我们'

 求主怜悯，
 求基督怜悯，
 求主怜悯。

9. The Hymn of Praise, Gloria in excelsis. It may be omitted during Advent and Lent.

Glory to God in the highest,
and peace to God's people on earth.
Lord God, heavenly King,
almighty God and Father,
    we worship you, we give you thanks,
    we praise you for your glory.
Lord Jesus Christ, only Son of the Father,
    Lord God, Lamb of God,
    you take away the sin of the world:
    have mercy on us;
    you are seated at the right hand of the Father:
    receive our prayer.
For you alone are the Holy One,
you alone are the Lord,
you alone are the Most High
    Jesus Christ,
    with the Holy Spirit,
    in the glory of God the Father. Amen.

10. Especially during Advent and Lent, the following (Trisagion) may be said.

Holy God, holy and mighty, holy and immortal,

have mercy on us.

11. The Collect of the Day

The priest says

    Let us pray.

The community may pray silently.

The priest says or sings the collect.

9. 荣耀主颂 降临节和大斋期可不用。

  惟愿在至高之处，荣耀归于上帝，
  在地上平安归于他的子民。
  主上帝，天上的王，
  全能的上帝圣父。
  我们敬拜你，感谢你，
  为你的荣耀称颂你，
  主耶稣基督，圣父的独生圣子，
  主上帝，上帝的羔羊，
  除掉世人罪的主：
  怜悯我们；
  坐在圣父右边的主：
  应允我们的祷告.
  因为惟有基督是圣，
  惟有基督是主，
  惟有耶稣基督和圣灵，
  在上帝圣父的荣耀里，
  同为至上。阿们。

10. 在降临节和大斋期，主礼可宣告：

  圣洁的，大能永恒的上帝怜悯我们。

11. 本日祝文 (可参考英文版公祷书)

主礼说，让我们祷告。

  会众可以默祷。

主礼选读或唱本日祝文。

THE MINISTRY OF THE WORD

12. All sit for the Reading from the Old Testament or as appointed.

After each reading the reader may say

Hear the word of the Lord,

> **thanks be to God.**

Silence may follow each reading.

13. A Psalm, hymn or anthem may be sung.

14. The Reading from the New Testament (other than from the gospels).

15. A hymn or anthem may be sung.

16. All stand for the Gospel Reading.

The deacon or other reader may say

> The Lord be with you.
> **And also with you.**

The reader says

> The Gospel of our Lord Jesus Christ according to [chapter... verse...].
> **Glory to you Lord Jesus Christ.**

After the Gospel, the reader says

> This is the Gospel of the Lord,
> **praise to you Lord Jesus Christ.**

Or

> [For] the Gospel of the Lord,
> **praise to you Lord Jesus Christ.**

17. The Sermon

Silence may follow.

圣言职事

12. 会众静坐聆听本日旧约经文。

读经者说 –

> 聆听上帝的话,
> **感谢上帝。**

每次读经后安静,默想。

13. 诵读诗篇,或唱圣诗。

14. 宣读新约书信

15. 诗歌

16. 全体起立聆听福音书

会吏或其他读经者说,

> 主与你们同在,
> **也与你同在**

会吏或其他读经者说,

> 我们主耶稣基督的福音,是记载在＿＿＿＿书,第＿＿＿＿章,第＿＿＿＿到第＿＿＿＿节,
> **荣耀归於主耶稣基督。**

福音书读毕后:

> 这是主耶稣的福音书,
> **愿赞美归於主耶稣基督。**

17. 讲道

安静默想

18. On Sundays the Nicene Creed below, or the Apostles' Creed on page 40, is said or sung, all standing.

The minister may say these or similar words.

Let us together affirm the faith of the Church:
We believe in one God,
   the Father, the almighty,
   maker of heaven and earth,
   of all that is, seen and unseen.
We believe in one Lord, Jesus Christ,
   the only Son of God,
   eternally begotten of the Father,
   God from God, Light from Light,
   true God from true God,
   begotten, not made,
   of one being with the Father;
   through him all things were made.
   For us and for our salvation
   he came down from heaven,
   was incarnate of the Holy Spirit and the virgin Mary
   and became truly human.
   For our sake he was crucified under Pontius Pilate;
   he suffered death and was buried.
   On the third day he rose again
   in accordance with the Scriptures;
   he ascended into heaven
   and is seated at the right hand of the Father.
   He will come again in glory to judge
   the living and the dead
   and his kingdom will have no end.
We believe in the Holy Spirit, the Lord, the giver of life, who proceeds from the Father and the Son,
   who with the Father and the Son
   is worshipped and glorified,
   who has spoken through the prophets.

18. 全体起立，宣读尼西亚或使徒信经（41页）

（主礼：让我们宣扬教会的信仰）

我们信独一上帝，全能的圣父，创造天地、并一切有形无形，万物的主。

我们信独一的主耶稣基督，上帝的独生子，在万世以前为圣父所生，从上帝所出的上帝，从光所出的光，从真神所出的真神，受生的，不是被造的，与父一体的。

万物都是藉着祂受造。他为要拯救我们世人，从天降临。

因圣灵的大能，为童贞女马利亚所生，道成肉身，在本丢彼拉多手下，为我们钉在十字架上，受害，受死，埋葬。

应验了圣经的话，
第三天复活，升天，
坐在圣父的右边。

将来必在荣耀中再临，
审判活人死人，
祂的国永无穷尽。

我信圣灵，赐生命的主，
从圣父、圣子所出，与圣父、圣子同受敬拜，同享尊荣。

昔日藉众先知传话。

We believe in one holy catholic and apostolic Church.
We acknowledge one baptism for the
 forgiveness of sins.
We look for the resurrection of the dead,
and the life of the world to come. Amen.

THE PRAYERS OF THE PEOPLE

19. The minister says

Let us pray for the world and for the Church.

The prayers may be offered by a deacon and/or members of the congregation.

Periods of silence may be kept.

Intercessions and thanksgivings may end with an appropriate response,
 for example:

Lord, in your mercy, Let us pray to the Lord.
hear our prayer. Lord, have mercy.
Lord, hear us. For your love and goodness
Lord, hear our prayer. we give you thanks, O God.
Father, hear our prayer God of grace,
through Jesus Christ our Lord. hear our prayer.

For suitable patterns of prayer, see pages 102–104

The prayers may conclude with this or another suitable prayer.
Almighty God, you have promised to hear our prayers.
Grant that what we have asked in faith
we may by your grace receive,
through Jesus Christ our Lord. Amen.

我们信使徒所传唯一圣而公之教会。

我们承认为赦罪而设的独一洗礼。

**我们盼望死人的复活,
并来世的永生。** 阿们。

19. 总祷文

主礼:

我们要为世界和教会祈祷。

也可以由一位会吏和其他会众祷告。祷告之间可以有间断,或静默。

感恩和代祷可以用以下合适的回应:

主阿, 求你怜悯, **垂听我们的祷告。**
让我们向主祈祷, **主阿,求你怜悯。**

合适的祷文,参考103-105页。

祷告可以用以下或其他合适的祷告结束:

全能的上帝, 你应许垂听我们的祷告.
求你应允我们凭信心献上的祷告,奉我们主耶稣基督的名求。阿们。

Or, unless the Lord's Prayer is used later, the minister may say

Accept our prayers through Jesus Christ our Lord, who taught us to pray,
Our Father in heaven,
   hallowed be your name,
   your kingdom come,
   your will be done,
   on earth as in heaven.
Give us today our daily bread.
Forgive us our sins
   as we forgive those who sin against us.
Save us from the time of trial
   and deliver us from evil.
For the kingdom, the power, and the glory are yours
now and for ever. Amen.

（除非主祷文将在后面使用）

主礼：

现在遵照我们主耶稣基督的教训，我们祷告说：

我们在天上的父，愿人都尊你的名为圣。
愿你的国降临。愿你的旨意行在地上，
如同行在天上。我们日用的饮食，今日赐给我们。
饶恕我们的罪，如同我们饶恕得罪我们的人。
不叫我们遇见试探，救我们脱离凶恶。
因为国度、权柄、荣耀，全是你的，
直到永远，阿们。

PREPARATION

20. A selection from the following or other suitable sentences of Scripture may be used.

Jesus said: Come to me all who labour and are heavy laden, and I will give you rest.
Matthew 11.28

Jesus said: I am the bread of life. Whoever comes to me will never be hungry, and whoever believes in me will never be thirsty.
John 6.35

Jesus said: A new commandment I give to you, that you love one another, even as I have loved you.
John 13.34

Whenever you stand praying, forgive, if you have anything against any one; so that your Father also who is in heaven may forgive you your trespasses.
Mark 11.25

God so loved the world that he gave his only Son, that whoever believes in him should not perish but have eternal life.
John 3.16

And/or

21. This Prayer of Approach may be used.

[Let us pray.]

We do not presume
to come to your table, merciful Lord,
trusting in our own righteousness,
but in your manifold and great mercies.
We are not worthy
so much as to gather up the crumbs under your table.
But you are the same Lord
whose nature is always to have mercy.
Grant us, therefore, gracious Lord,
so to eat the flesh of your dear Son Jesus Christ,
and to drink his blood,
that we may evermore dwell in him,
and he in us. Amen.

预备圣餐

20. 选择以下或其他合适的经文

   耶稣说:"凡劳苦担重担的人, 可以到我这里来, 我就使你们得安息。"(太11.28)

   耶稣说:「我就是生命的粮。到我这里来的,必定不饿;信我的,永远不渴。(约6:35)

   我赐给你们一条新命令,乃是叫你们彼此相爱;我怎样爱你们,你们也要怎样相爱。(约13:34)

   你们站着祷告的时候,若想起有人得罪你们,就当饶恕他,好叫你们在天上的父也饶恕你们的过犯。(可11:25)

   上帝爱世人,甚至将他的独生子赐给他们,叫一切信他的,不致灭亡,反得永生。(约3:16)

21. 谦恭近主文

   (让我们同心祷告)
   最慈悲的主,我们到你圣桌前,不敢靠自己的功劳,
   惟靠你无限量的恩惠。

   我们就是捡你圣桌下的零碎,也是不配的,惟你是不改变的主,常怀怜悯的心,求恩主帮助我们,
   能领受爱子耶稣基督的圣体宝血,使我们常在他里面,
   他也常在我们里面。阿们。

CONFESSION AND ABSOLUTION

22. At least on Sundays and other Holy Days a general Confession is said here if it has not been said at ¶ 6.

The deacon or other minister introduces the confession with the following, a seasonal introduction or other suitable words such as an exhortation, 1 Corinthians 11.26–28 or Isaiah 55.6–8.

God is steadfast in love and infinite in mercy, welcoming sinners and inviting them to the Lord's table.

Silence may be kept.

Let us confess our sins in penitence and faith, confident in God's forgiveness.
**Merciful God,
our maker and our judge,
we have sinned against you in thought, word, and deed,
and in what we have failed to do:
we have not loved you with our whole heart;
we have not loved our neighbours as ourselves;
we repent, and are sorry for all our sins.
Father, forgive us.
Strengthen us to love and obey you in newness of life;
through Jesus Christ our Lord. Amen.**

23. The Absolution. Standing, the priest says

Almighty God,
who has promised forgiveness to all who turn to him in faith:
pardon you and set you free from all your sins,
strengthen you in all goodness
and keep you in eternal life,
through Jesus Christ our Lord. **Amen.**

认罪和赦罪

22. （在主日和其他圣日，此认罪文若不是在*6已使用，请在这里认罪。）

会吏和其他传道人可按教会年历，或其他合适的祷告文，的经文，如歌林多前书11.26-28，或以赛亚书55.6-8.带领会众认罪。

　　上帝有永恒不变的慈爱和怜悯，他欢迎罪人到圣桌前来。

会众保持静默

　　让我们以谦卑信靠的心，并确信上帝的赦免。
　　慈悲的上帝，
　　创造和审判我们的主，我们得罪了你。
　　我们承认在思想，言语和行为上，常常得罪了祢；
　　应做的不做，不应做的反去做。
　　我们没有尽心爱祢；也没有爱人如己。
　　现在我们痛心懊悔，
　　恳求祢施怜悯，因着圣子我们主耶稣基督，
　　饶恕我们的已往，扶助我们的现在，引导我们的将来；
　　好叫我们乐意遵行你的旨意，蒙你悦纳，
　　而归荣耀给祢的圣名。阿们。

23. 赦罪文　牧师起立说：

　　全能的上帝应许，藉着我们主耶稣基督，凭信心来到他面前求赦罪的，必得着赦免，从罪中得释放。主必增强你们行善的力量，保守你们进入永生。**阿门。**

THE GREETING OF PEACE

24. All stand. The Greeting of Peace is introduced with these or other suitable words.

We are the body of Christ.
His Spirit is with us.

Or

Christ has reconciled us to God in one body by the cross.
We meet in his name and share his peace.

The priest says

The peace of the Lord be always with you.
And also with you.

All may exchange a sign of peace.

A hymn may be sung.

25. The gifts of the people are brought to the Lord's Table. They may be presented in silence or a suitable prayer, such as the following, may be used.

Blessed are you, Lord, God of all creation.
Through your goodness we have these gifts to share.
Accept and use our offerings for your glory
and for the service of your kingdom.
Blessed be God for ever.

平安礼

24. 平安礼 （全体起立）

牧师说：

> 我们是基督的身体，
> **他的圣灵与我们同在。**

或

> 基督透过十字架与我们联合，使我们与上帝和好，
> **我们在他的名里相遇，并分享他的平安。**
> 启：愿主的平安与你们同在。
> **也与你同在。**

此时，牧师及会众可奉主的名互相请安。

奉献诗歌

25. 会众的奉献可放到圣桌上，保持安静，可用以下的祷文。

（会众肃立）

> 創造萬有的主上帝，我們讚美你，因着你的恩惠，我们能将礼物献上。
> 求你悦纳我们的奉献，使用在你国度的事工，来荣耀你的名。
> **愿赞美永远归於上帝。**

THE GREAT THANKSGIVING

26. The priest takes the bread and wine for the communion, places them on the Lord's Table, and says the following (Thanksgiving 1) or another authorised Prayer of Thanksgiving and Consecration.

Additional Thanksgivings (A Prayer Book for Australia)
Thanksgiving 2 (page 130)
Thanksgiving 3 (page 133)
Thanksgiving 4 (page 136)
Thanksgiving 5 (page 139)
The Great Thanksgiving (Third Order) on page 104 of this book.

Thanksgiving 1
[The Lord be with you.
And also with you.]
Lift up your hearts.
We lift them to the Lord.
Let us give thanks to the Lord our God.
It is right to give our thanks and praise.

A Seasonal Preface may be substituted for 'All glory and honour ... saying:'

All glory and honour be yours always and everywhere,
  mighty Creator, everliving God.
We give you thanks and praise for our Saviour Jesus Christ,
  who by the power of your Spirit was born of Mary
  and lived as one of us.
By his death on the cross
  and rising to new life,
  he offered the one true sacrifice for sin
  and obtained an eternal deliverance for his people.

大祝谢文

26. 牧师预备圣餐的饼和酒，放在圣桌上，说以下（第一祝谢礼文）或其他教会认可的祝谢文和祝圣文。

祝谢文2-5，请参考英文版公祷书130页

大祝谢文 （第三套程序）在105页

第一祝谢文

启：愿主与你们同在　　**应：愿主也与你同在。**

启：你们心里当仰望主。　**应：我们心里仰望主。**

启：我们应当感谢我主上帝。**应：感谢我主上帝是应当的。**

一段合适的节期序言可取代"全能的创造者。。。常赞美你说："

全能的创造者，永生的上帝，
无论何时何地， 一切荣耀和尊贵，
全归于你。
我们献上感恩和赞美，
是因我们的救主耶稣基督，
因圣灵的大能，为童贞女马利亚所生，道成肉身，
藉着在十字架上的死和复活，
他成就了一个完全的赎罪祭，为属他的人成就了永恒的拯救。

Therefore with angels and archangels,
    and with all the company of heaven,
    we proclaim your great and glorious name,
    for ever praising you and saying:
    Holy, holy, holy Lord, God of power and might,
    Heaven and earth are full of your glory.
    Hosanna in the highest.
    [Blessed is he who comes in the name of the Lord.
    Hosanna in the highest.]

Merciful God, we thank you
    for these gifts of your creation,
    this bread and wine,
    and we pray that by your Word and Holy Spirit,
    we who eat and drink them
    may be partakers of Christ's body and blood.

On the night he was betrayed Jesus took bread;
    and when he had given you thanks
    he broke it, and gave it to his disciples, saying,
    'Take, eat. This is my body given for you.
    Do this in remembrance of me.'

After supper, he took the cup,
    and again giving you thanks
    he gave it to his disciples, saying,
    'Drink from this, all of you.
    This is my blood of the new covenant
    shed for you and for many
    for the forgiveness of sins.
    Do this, as often as you drink it, in remembrance of me.'

因此，我们与天使和天使长，天上的会众，
一同称赞颂扬你伟大和荣耀的圣名，
常赞美你说：
圣哉，圣哉，圣哉，天地万军的主上帝，
你的荣光充满天地。
奉主名而来的，当受赞美！
在至高之处，亦当称颂主！
仁慈的上帝，
我们为你所创造的礼物 – 这饼和酒感谢你，
求你藉着你道和圣灵的力量，当我们领受这饼和酒时，
就能同享基督的身体和宝血。
主耶稣被卖的那一夜，拿起饼来，
祝谢了，就擘开，分给他的门徒，说：
 "你们拿这个吃，这是我的身体，
是为你们舍的；你们应该这样行，以纪念我。"
饭后，祂也照样拿起杯来，
祝谢了，递给门徒，说：
 "你们都拿这个喝，
这杯是用我的血所立的新约，
为你们和众人，为赦罪流的。
你们每次喝的时候，应该这样行，以纪念我。"

The memorial acclamation is used here or below.

**Christ has died.
Christ is risen.
Christ will come again.**
Therefore we do as our Saviour has commanded:
    proclaiming his offering of himself
    made once for all upon the cross,
    his mighty resurrection and glorious ascension,
    and looking for his coming again,
    we celebrate, with this bread and this cup,
    his one perfect and sufficient sacrifice
    for the sins of the whole world.

The memorial acclamation may be used here.

Renew us by your Holy Spirit,
unite us in the body of your Son,
and bring us with all your people
into the joy of your eternal kingdom;
    through Jesus Christ our Lord,
with whom, and in whom,
in the fellowship of the Holy Spirit,
we worship you, Father,
in songs of never-ending praise:
**Blessing and honour and glory and power
are yours for ever and ever. Amen.**

因此我们要宣扬信仰的奥秘，说：

牧师和会众同心颂读：

基督曾经受死，
基督现已复活，
基督将要再临。

因此，我们按着主的命令：
宣扬祂在十字架上，为所有的人，把自己献上，
祂已复活，并荣耀地升天，
我们期待祂的再来。

我们以这饼和杯，感谢祂为全世界的罪，一次献上满足完全的赎罪祭。

求圣灵更新我们，使我们与你的圣子合一，
带领我们和你的子民一同进入你永恒喜乐的国度；
奉我们主耶稣基督的名，并在圣灵的团契中，我们敬拜你，永远歌颂赞美你：

颂赞、尊贵、荣耀、权柄全是你的，直到永远。阿们。

27. If the Lord's Prayer has not already been said, it is said here or after the communion. The priest says

As our Saviour Christ has taught us, we are confident to pray,
Our Father in heaven,
 hallowed be your name,
 your kingdom come,
 your will be done,
 on earth as in heaven.
Give us today our daily bread.
Forgive us our sins
 as we forgive those who sin against us.
Save us from the time of trial
 and deliver us from evil.
For the kingdom, the power, and the glory are yours
 now and for ever. Amen.

THE BREAKING OF THE BREAD AND THE COMMUNION

28. The priest breaks the bread. One of the following may be said.

[We break this bread to share in the body of Christ.]
We who are many are one body,
 for we all share in the one bread.

Or

As this broken bread was once many grains,
which have been gathered together and made one bread:
 so may your Church be gathered
 from the ends of the earth into your kingdom.

29. The priest and other communicants receive the Holy Communion.

The sacrament is given with the following words.

27. 如果尚未用**主祷文**祷告，牧师在这里或圣餐后说：

我们的救主耶稣基督曾教导我们这样祷告：

我们在天上的父，
愿人都尊你的名为圣。
愿你的国降临。
愿你的旨意行在地上，
如同行在天上。
我们日用的饮食，今日赐给我们。
饶恕我们的罪，如同我们饶恕得罪我们的人。
不叫我们遇见试探，救我们脱离凶恶。
因为国度、权柄、荣耀，全是你的，
直到永远，阿们。

擘饼和圣餐

28. 牧师在此擘饼

我們雖众，仍属一体，
   因为我們都是分享這餅。

或

这擘开的饼本是很多麦子，在一起成为了这饼：
愿你的教会从地极一同聚集，进入你的国度。

29. 分发圣餐 分发者可说：

The body of our Lord Jesus Christ, which was given for you, preserve your body and soul to everlasting life. Take and eat this in remembrance that Christ died for you, and feed on him in your heart by faith with thanksgiving.

And

The blood of our Lord Jesus Christ, which was shed for you, preserve your body and soul to everlasting life. Drink this in remembrance that Christ's blood was shed for you, and be thankful.

Or, the priest says

[The gifts of God for the people of God.]

Come let us take this holy sacrament of the body and blood of Christ in remembrance that he died for us, and feed on him in our hearts by faith with thanksgiving.

The sacrament is given with the following words, after which the communicant responds, Amen.

The body of Christ [the bread of heaven] keep you in eternal life. **Amen.**

The blood of Christ [the cup of salvation] keep you in eternal life. **Amen.**

> 我们主耶稣基督的身体，为你而舍，保守你的身体和灵魂进入永生。以感恩和信心领受这饼，记念基督为你受死。

和

> 我们主耶稣基督的宝血，为你而流，保守你的身体和灵魂进入永生。以感恩的心领受这杯，记念基督为你流血。

或

牧师说：

> 前来领受这圣礼，以记念耶稣基督为我们而死。以信心和感恩的心前来领受。

分发时可说：

> 基督的身体（天上的粮），保守你进入永生。**阿们！**
> 基督的宝血（救恩的杯），保守你进入永生。**阿们！**

THE SENDING OUT OF GOD'S PEOPLE

30. The priest says one of the following or another suitable prayer

   a Gracious God,
>   we thank you that in this sacrament
>   you assure us of your goodness and love.
>   Accept our sacrifice of praise and thanksgiving
>   and help us to grow in love and obedience
>   that we may serve you in the world
>   and finally be brought to that table
>   where all your saints feast with you for ever.

Or

   b Bountiful God,
>   at this table you graciously feed us
>   with the bread of life and the cup of eternal salvation.
>   May we who have reached out our hands to receive
>   this sacrament
>   be strengthened in your service;
>   we who have sung your praises
>   tell of your glory and truth in our lives;
>   we who have seen the greatness of your love
>   see you face to face in your kingdom
>   and come to worship you with all your saints for ever.

Or

   c Living God,
>   in this holy meal you fill us with new hope.
>   May the power of your love,
>   which we have known in word and sacrament,
>   continue your saving work among us,
>   give us courage for our pilgrimage,
>   and bring us to the joys you promise.

差遣

30. 牧师宣读以下一段祷文或配合节期的祷文。

> 让我们一同祷告：
> 慈悲的上帝，
> 我们感谢你在这圣礼中使我们确定你的良善和慈爱。
> 求你悦纳我们献上的赞美和感恩，
> 帮助我们在爱和顺服中成长，
> 以至我们可以在世界服侍你，
> 并在最后被领到你与众圣徒聚餐的桌前，直到永远。

或

> 慷慨的上帝，
> 在这圣桌旁，你用生命的灵粮和永恒救恩的福杯喂养了我们。
> 愿我们这些伸手领受圣礼的人能被你坚固；
> 那些唱出对你赞美的，能在生活中诉说你的荣耀与真理。
> 那些看见你大爱的，能在你的国度里与你面对面，
> 并得以与众圣徒一同敬拜你直到永远。

或

> 永活的上帝，
> 在这圣餐中你以新的希望充满我们。
> 愿我们在圣言与圣礼中所领受你爱的大能，
> 继续在我们中间施行拯救的大工，
> 赐我们勇气走天路，
> 并带领我们进入你所应许的喜乐中。

Or

d Father of all
>we give you thanks and praise
>that when we were still far off
>you met us in your Son and brought us home.

>Dying and living, he declared your love,
>gave us grace, and opened the gate of glory.
>May we who share Christ's body live his risen life;
>we who drink his cup bring life to others;
>we whom the Spirit lights give light to the world.
>**Keep us in this hope that we have grasped;**
>**so we and all your children shall be free,**
>**and the whole earth live to praise your name.**

If this prayer is said, ¶ 31 may be omitted.

或

众人的父
我们感谢你,敬拜你。
当我们仍在远离你的时候,你在圣子里与我们相遇并带领我们回家。
通过死亡和生命,他宣告你的爱,
赐我们恩典,并开启了荣耀的大门。
愿我们这些分享基督的身体的人,能活出祂复活的生命。
喝祂的杯的人,能给他人带来生命。
被圣灵光照的人,能照亮世界。
让我们常活在已经得到的盼望中,
使我们和你所有的儿女都得自由,全地都要活泼地赞美你的名。

31. All say together, either

> Father,
> **we offer ourselves to you**
> **as a living sacrifice**
> **through Jesus Christ our Lord.**
> **Send us out in the power of your Spirit**
> **to live and work to your praise and glory.**

Or

> Most loving God,
> **you send us into the world you love.**
> **Give us grace to go thankfully and with courage**
> **in the power of your Spirit.**

32. A hymn may be sung.

33. The priest says this or an appropriate seasonal Blessing.

> The peace of God which passes all understanding keep your hearts and minds in the knowledge and love of God, and of his Son, Jesus Christ our Lord;
>
> and the blessing of God almighty, the Father, the Son, and the Holy Spirit, be among you and remain with you always. **Amen.**

34. The deacon may say

> Go in peace to love and serve the Lord:
>> **In the name of Christ. Amen**

Or

> Go in the peace of Christ.
>> **Thanks be to God.**

During the Easter season 'Alleluia, alleluia' may be added to the dismissal and the people's response.

31. 全体说：

> 天父，
> **我们奉耶稣基督的名，把自己当作活祭献上。**
> **差遣我们带着圣灵的能力出去，在生活和工作上，把赞美和荣耀都归给你。**

或

> 最慈爱的上帝，
> **差遣我们出去你所爱的世界中。赐给我们圣灵的力量，带着感恩和信心出去。**

32. 唱诗

33. 牧师用以下或其他合宜的祝福文，说

> 愿上帝所赐出人意外的平安，保守你们的心怀意念，
> 使你们晓得敬爱上帝和祂的圣子，我们主耶稣基督。
> 又愿全能的上帝，圣父，圣子，圣灵赐福给你们，直到永远。
> **阿门。**

34. 会吏说，

> 启：你们要平平安安地去敬爱主，服侍主。
> **应：奉基督的名。阿门。**

或

> 启：愿基督的平安与你同去，
> **应： 感谢上帝。**

在复活节期间，在散会时或可加上"哈里路亚！"，
  会众的回应是："哈里路亚！"

THE HOLY COMMUNION THIRD ORDER

GATHERING IN GOD'S NAME

1. The priest greets the people. The service may begin with songs or hymns of praise and thanksgiving.

2. The minister says this or another suitable Sentence of Scripture.

    Our Lord Jesus Christ said:

    You shall love the Lord your God with all your heart, and with all your soul, and with all your mind, and with all your strength. This is the great and first commandment. And a second is like it: You shall love your neighbour as yourself. On these two commandments hang all the law and the prophets.

    Matthew 22.37–40, Mark 12.30–31

    Let us pray.
    **Almighty God,
    to whom all hearts are open,
    all desires known,
    and from whom no secrets are hidden:
    cleanse the thoughts of our hearts
    by the inspiration of your Holy Spirit,
    that we may perfectly love you,
    and worthily magnify your holy name,
    through Christ our Lord. Amen.**

3. 'Glory to God in the Highest' or some other hymn of praise may be sung.

4. The Collect of the Day

圣餐崇拜
程序三

奉上帝的名聚会

1. 牧师向众人问安

诗歌

2. 主礼宣读以下，或合适的礼文

> 我们的主耶稣基督说：'你要尽心、尽性、尽意、尽力、爱主你的上帝，这是第一最大的诫命，其次爱人如己也是这样。这两条诫命是律法和先知一切道理的总纲。(太22:37-40, 可12:30-31)
>
> 让我们祷告：
> **全能的上帝，凡人的心，在主面前无不显明，**
> **心里所羡慕的，主都知道，**
> **心里所隐藏的，也瞒不过主。**
> **求主用圣灵的感化，洁净我们心里的意念，**
> **使我们尽心爱主，恭敬归荣耀与主的圣名。**
> **这都是靠着我们的主耶稣基督。**
> **阿们。**

3. 诗歌

4. 本日祝文

THE MINISTRY OF THE WORD

5. The Bible readings follow, one from the Old Testament and one or two from the New Testament. A reading from the Gospels is always included.

After each reading the reader may say

Hear the word of the Lord,
thanks be to God.

6. A psalm or portion of a psalm may be sung or said and a suitable hymn or song may follow any of the readings.

7. All stand for the Gospel reading.

The reader may say

The Gospel of our Lord Jesus Christ according to…
[chapter… verse…]
Glory to you Lord Jesus Christ.

After the Gospel, the reader says

This is the Gospel of the Lord,

Or

[For] the Gospel of the Lord,
praise to you Lord Jesus Christ.

8. The Sermon is preached here or after the creed.

圣言职事

5. 宣读圣经（旧约、新约）

每次读完，可用以下做回应

    聆听上帝的道。
    感谢上帝。

6. 颂读诗篇/诗歌

7. 宣读福音书（全体起立）

宣读者可以这样开始：

    我们主耶稣基督的福音，是记载在____书，第____章，第____到第____节，
    荣耀归於主耶稣基督
    …

福音书读毕後：

    这是主的福音，
    赞美归於主耶稣基督。

8. 在此，或宣读使徒信经後讲道

9. On Sundays the Nicene Creed below, or the Apostles' Creed on page 40, is said or sung, all standing.

> We believe in one God,
>   the Father, the almighty,
>   maker of heaven and earth,
>   of all that is, seen and unseen.
> We believe in one Lord, Jesus Christ,
>   the only Son of God,
>   eternally begotten of the Father,
>   God from God, Light from Light,
>   true God from true God,
>   begotten, not made,
>   of one being with the Father;
>   through him all things were made.
>   For us and for our salvation
>   he came down from heaven,
>   was incarnate of the Holy Spirit and the virgin Mary
>   and became truly human.
>   For our sake he was crucified under Pontius Pilate;
>   he suffered death and was buried.
>   On the third day he rose again
>   in accordance with the Scriptures;
>   he ascended into heaven
>   and is seated at the right hand of the Father.
>   He will come again in glory to judge
>   the living and the dead
>   and his kingdom will have no end.
> We believe in the Holy Spirit, the Lord, the giver of life,
>   who proceeds from the Father and the Son,
>   who with the Father and the Son
>   is worshipped and glorified,
>   who has spoken through the prophets.
>   We believe in one holy catholic and apostolic Church.
>   We acknowledge one baptism for the forgiveness of sins.
>   We look for the resurrection of the dead,
>   and the life of the world to come. Amen.

9. 主日中全体起立宣读

我们信独一上帝，全能的圣父，创造天地、并一切有形无形，万物的主。
我们信独一的主耶稣基督，上帝的独生子，在万世以前为圣父所生，从上帝所出的上帝，从光所出的光，从真神所出的真神，受生的，不是被造的，与父一体的。
万物都是藉着祂受造。他为要拯救我们世人，从天降临。
因圣灵的大能，为童贞女马利亚所生，道成肉身，在本丢彼拉多手下，为我们钉在十字架上，受害，受死，埋葬。
应验了圣经的话，
第三天复活，升天，
坐在圣父的右边。
将来必在荣耀中再临，
审判活人死人，
祂的国永无穷尽。
我信圣灵， 赐生命的主，
从圣父、圣子所出，与圣父、圣子同受敬拜，同享尊荣。
昔日藉众先知传话。
我们信使徒所传唯一圣而公之教会。
我们承认为赦罪而设的独一洗礼。
我们盼望死人的复活，
并来世的永生。 阿们。

Or

I believe in God, the Father almighty,
   creator of heaven and earth.
I believe in Jesus Christ, God's only Son, our Lord,
   who was conceived by the Holy Spirit,
   born of the virgin Mary,
   suffered under Pontius Pilate,
   was crucified, died, and was buried;
   he descended to the dead.
   On the third day he rose from the dead;
   he ascended into heaven,
   and is seated at the right hand of the Father;
   from there he will come to judge
   the living and the dead.
I believe in the Holy Spirit,
   the holy catholic Church,
   the communion of saints,
   the forgiveness of sins,
   the resurrection of the body,
   and the life everlasting. Amen.

10. The Sermon is preached here if it has not been preached earlier.

11. A hymn or song may follow.

或

> 我信上帝，全能的父，创造天地的主；
> 我信我主耶稣基督，上帝独生的子；
> 因圣灵感孕，由童贞女马利亚所生，
> 在本丢彼拉多手下受难，被钉于十字架，受死，埋葬；降在阴间；
> 第三天从死人中复活；升天，坐在全能父上帝的右边；
> 将来必从那里降临，审判活人死人。
> 我信圣灵，
> 我信圣而公之教会；
> 我信圣徒相通；
> 我信罪得赦免；
> 我信身体复活；
> 我信永生。 阿们。

10. 讲道（如果之前没有讲道）

11. 诗歌

THE PRAYERS OF THE PEOPLE

12. One or more members of the congregation may pray, using this form or a suitable alternative.

Almighty God, your Son Jesus Christ has promised that you will hear us when we ask in faith: receive the prayers we offer.

For the nations

We give thanks for... We pray for...

Guide with your wisdom and power the leaders of the nations, so that everyone may live in peace and mutual trust, sharing with justice the resources of the earth. Give the people of this land a spirit of unselfishness, compassion, and fairness in public and private life.

Father, hear our prayer
through Jesus Christ our Lord.

Or

Lord, in your mercy
hear our prayer.

For the Church

We give thanks for... We pray for...

Send out the light and truth of your gospel and bring people everywhere to know and love you. Enable those who minister among us to commend your truth by their example and teaching. May we gladly receive and obey your word.

Father, hear our prayer
through Jesus Christ our Lord.

Or

Lord, in your mercy
hear our prayer.

For those in need

We give thanks for... We pray for...

We commend to your fatherly care, merciful God, all who are in sorrow, sickness, discouragement or any other trouble. Give them patience and a firm trust in your goodness.

祷告

12. 一个或更多的会众参与祷告，可用以下模式，或其他合适方法。
国家祷可用以下，或合适的祷文

    全能的上帝，你的儿子耶稣基督应允我们，若以信心向你祈求，你必垂听。求你垂听我们现在献上的祷告。

为国家祷告

    我们为____献上感恩…，我们为____祷告…。
    求你赐智慧和能力给各国的领袖们，使所有人都能生活在和平和互信的环境中，公平地分享地上的资源。赐给这地的人民，不论是在公众或是私人的生活，都有无私、怜悯和公平的心灵。
    天父，垂听我们的祷告。
    奉我们主耶稣基督的名求。阿们！

或

    求主怜悯，
    垂听我们的祷告。

为教会祷告

    我们为____献上感恩…，我们为____祷告…。
    求主赐下福音的真理和亮光，使更多的人能认识你和敬爱你。求主使在我们当中的牧者能以自己作榜样，正确地教导你的真理。
    愿我们乐意接受并遵行你的话语。
    天父，垂听我们的祷告。
    奉我们主耶稣基督的名求。阿们！

或

    求主怜悯，
    垂听我们的祷告

为有需要的人祷告

    我们为____献上感恩…，我们为____祷告…。
    慈悲的上帝，我们把那些正在悲伤中、疾病中、情绪低落和在不同困难中的人交托给你，求你赐给他们忍耐和信靠的心。

Help those who care for them, and bring us all into the joy of your salvation.

Father, hear our prayer
through Jesus Christ our Lord.

Or

Lord, in your mercy
hear our prayer.

Thanksgiving for the faithful departed

We give thanks for the life and work of…

We praise you for all your servants whose lives have honoured Christ. Encourage us by their example, so that we may run with perseverance the race that lies before us, and share with them the fullness of joy in your kingdom.

The prayers conclude with

Hear us, Father,
through Jesus Christ our Lord,
who lives and reigns with you
in the unity of the Holy Spirit,
one God, now and for ever. Amen.

Or

Accept our prayers through Jesus Christ our Lord, who taught us to pray,
Our Father in heaven,
hallowed be your name,
your kingdom come,
your will be done,
on earth as in heaven.
Give us today our daily bread.
Forgive us our sins
as we forgive those who sin against us.
Save us from the time of trial
and deliver us from evil.
For the kingdom, the power, and the glory are yours
now and for ever. Amen.

也求你帮助那些关心他们的人，让我们都进入你救恩的喜乐中。
天父，垂听我们的祷告。
奉我们主耶稣基督的名求。阿们！

或

求主怜悯，
垂听我们的祷告

为离世的忠心信徒感恩

我们为＿＿＿＿献上感恩...，我们为＿＿＿＿祷告...。
我们为那些在生命中荣耀基督的仆人们来赞美你。让他们成为我们的榜样，以坚忍的心奔跑那摆在我們前面的路程，并与众人一同分享天国丰盛的喜乐。

结束祷告

天父，求你垂听我们的祷告。
奉我们主耶稣基督的名，
他永远活着，并与圣父和圣灵，统管万有，直到永远。阿们！

或

求主悦纳我们的祷告，奉我们主耶稣基督，那位曾经教导我们祷告，说：

**我们在天上的父，愿人都尊你的名为圣。
愿你的国降临。愿你的旨意行在地上，
如同行在天上。我们日用的饮食，今日赐给我们。
饶恕我们的罪，如同我们饶恕得罪我们的人。
不叫我们遇见试探，救我们脱离凶恶。
因为国度、权柄、荣耀，全是你的，
直到永远，阿们。**

PREPARATION FOR THE LORD'S SUPPER

13. One of the following or a suitable alternative may be read.
An exhortation may be read.

As often as you eat this bread and drink the cup, you proclaim the Lord's death until he comes. Whoever, therefore, eats the bread and drinks the cup of the Lord in an unworthy manner will be answerable for the body and blood of the Lord. Examine yourselves, and only then eat of the bread and drink of the cup.

1 Corinthians 11.26–28

Seek the Lord while he may be found, call upon him while he is near; let the wicked forsake their way, and the unrighteous their thoughts; let them return to the Lord, that he may have mercy on them, and to our God, for he will abundantly pardon. For my thoughts are not your thoughts, nor are your ways my ways, says the Lord.

Isaiah 55.6–8

We are God's children now, and what we will be has not yet been made known. But we know that when he appears we shall be like him, for we shall see him as he is. All who have this hope in him purify themselves, just as he is pure.

1 John 3.2–3

14. A time of silence may follow.

The deacon or other minister says

Knowing the goodness of God and our failure to respond with love and obedience, let us confess our sins, saying together,

Heavenly Father,
you have loved us with an everlasting love,
but we have broken your holy laws
and have left undone what we ought to have done.
We are sorry for our sins
   and turn away from them.
For the sake of your Son who died for us,
   forgive us, cleanse us and change us.

预备圣餐

13. 宣读以下一段，或其他合适的经文。可宣读一段劝勉的话语。

你们每逢吃这饼、喝这杯，是表明主的死，直等到他来。所以，无论何人，不按理吃主的饼、喝主的杯，就是干犯主的身、主的血了。人应当自己省察，然后吃这饼、喝这杯。

（林前11:26-28）

当趁耶和华可寻找的时候寻找他，相近的时候求告他。恶人当离弃自己的道路，不义的人当除掉自己的意念。归向耶和华，耶和华就必怜恤他；当归向我们的神，因为神必广行赦免。耶和华说："我的意念非同你们的意念，我的道路非同你们的道路。（赛55:6-8）

我们现在是神的儿女，将来如何，还未显明。但我们知道，主若显现，我们必要像他，因为必得见他的真体。³ 凡向他有这指望的，就洁净自己，像他洁净一样。

（约壹3:2-3）

14. 片刻安静

牧师说：

我们知道上帝的良善，却没有以爱和顺服来回应，让我们承认自己的罪，一同说：
天父，你用永恒不变的爱，来爱我们，
但我们却没有遵行你 的圣律法，
没有行我们应该行的，
我们为我们的罪深深懊悔，
愿意从 今悔改，因着为我们舍身的圣子，
赦免我们、洁净我们，并改变我们，

By your Holy Spirit,
> **enable us to live for you;**
> **through Jesus Christ our Lord. Amen.**

15. **The priest stands and declares God's forgiveness in these or other authorised words.**

God is slow to anger and full of compassion,
forgiving all who humbly repent
> and trust in his Son as Saviour and Lord.
God therefore forgives you in Christ Jesus,
in whom there is no condemnation. **Amen.**

One or more of the following passages may also be read as an assurance of God's forgiveness.

God so loved the world that he gave his only Son, so that everyone who believes in him may not perish but may have eternal life.

John 3.16

As far as the east is from the west, so far has God removed our sins from us.

Psalm 103.12

Our Lord Jesus Christ himself bore our sins in his body on the cross, so that we might die to sin and live for righteousness; by his wounds you have been healed.

1 Peter 2.24

THE GREETING OF PEACE

16. **All stand. The Greeting of Peace is introduced with these or other suitable words.**

We are the body of Christ.
> **His Spirit is with us.**

The priest says

The peace of the Lord be always with you.
> **And also with you.**

All may exchange a sign of peace.

17. **The gifts of the people are brought to the Lord's Table. A hymn or song may be sung.**

藉著圣灵，使我们为你而活；
奉我们的主耶稣基督的名，阿们。

15. 牧师用以下，或其他获授权的语句，宣告神的赦免。

上帝是满有怜悯，不轻易发怒，
赦免所有谦卑悔改并相信圣子为救主和主的人。
因此，上帝在基督耶稣里赦免你，不定你的罪。**阿们！**

可宣读一段或更多以下的经文，确认神的赦免。

上帝爱世人，甚至将他的独生子赐给他们，叫一切信他的不致灭亡，反得永生。(约3:16)
东离西有多远，他叫我们的过犯离我们也有多远。(诗103:12)
他被挂在木头上，亲身担当了我们的罪，使我们既然在罪上死，就得以在义上活。因他受的鞭伤，你们便得了医治。(彼前2:24)

问安

16. 全体起立。可用以下，或合适的话语问安。

我们是基督的身体。
祂的灵与我们同在。

牧师说：

愿主的平安常与你们同在。
也与你同在。

会众互相问安。

17. 奉献/诗歌

THE GREAT THANKSGIVING

> 18. Bread and the wine for the communion are placed on the Lord's Table. The priest says the following or another authorised Prayer of Thanksgiving and Consecration.

[The Lord be with you.
And also with you.]
Lift up your hearts.
We lift them to the Lord.
Let us give thanks to the Lord our God.
It is right to give our thanks and praise.
You are worthy, our Lord and God,
    to receive glory and honour and power,
    for you created all things,
    making us in your own image.
We praise you for your Son,
    our Saviour Jesus Christ,
    who by his death on the cross
    and rising to new life
    offered the one true sacrifice for sin
    and obtained an eternal deliverance for his people.
Therefore, we lift our voices to praise you, saying,
    Holy, holy, holy Lord, God of power and might,
    heaven and earth are full of your glory.
    Hosanna in the highest.
And now, gracious God, we thank you
    for these gifts of bread and wine,
    and pray that we who receive them,
    in the fellowship of the Holy Spirit,
    according to our Saviour's word,
    in remembrance of his suffering and death,
    may share his body and blood.

大祝谢文

18. 预备圣餐的饼和酒。牧师用以下或其他授权礼文作感恩和祝圣祷告。

主与你们同在。
也与你同在。
你们心里当仰望主。
我们心里仰望主。
我们应当感谢我主上帝。
感谢我主上帝是应当的。

我们的主,我们的上帝,你是配得荣耀、尊贵和权柄,
因为你创造了万物,并按着你的形象创造了我们。

我们感谢你,因着你的圣子,我们的救主耶稣基督,在十字架上的受死和复活,献上永远的赎罪祭,使属祂的人都得到永恒的救赎。

因此,我们一同高声赞美你,说:

**圣哉、圣哉、圣哉,天地万军的主上帝,
你的荣光充满天地。
奉主名而来的,当受赞美!
在至高之处,亦当称颂主!**
现在,恩慈的上帝,我们为这饼和酒献上感恩。
我们向你祈求,在圣灵中领受这饼和酒的人,就如我们救主所说,
一同记念祂的受苦和死亡时,都可以分享祂的身体和宝血。

On the night before he died, Jesus took bread,
   and when he had given you thanks
   he broke it, and gave it to his disciples, saying,
   'Take and eat. This is my body which is given for you.
   Do this in remembrance of me.'

If the bread is broken here, the priest may say

[We who are many are one body in Christ,
   for we all share in the one bread.]

After supper, he took the cup,
   and again giving you thanks
   he gave it to his disciples, saying,
   'Drink from this, all of you.
   This is my blood of the new covenant
   which is shed for you and for many
   for the forgiveness of sins.
   Do this, as often as you drink it, in remembrance of me.'

We eat this bread and drink this cup
   to proclaim the death of the Lord.
We do this until he returns.
   Come, Lord Jesus!
Father, as we recall his saving death and glorious resurrection,
   may we who share these gifts
   be renewed by your Holy Spirit
   and united in the body of your Son.
Bring us with all your people
   into the joy of your eternal kingdom,
   there to feast at your table and
   join in your eternal praise:
   Worthy is the Lamb, who was slain,
   to receive praise and honour
   and glory and power
   for ever and ever. Amen.

主耶稣被卖的那一夜,
拿起饼来,祝谢了,就擘开,分给他的门徒,
说:"你们拿这个吃,这是我的身体,
是为你们牺牲的;你们应该这样行,以记念我。"

擘饼

我们虽众,在基督里仍属一个身体,
因为我们都分享这饼。

饭后,他也照样拿起杯来,祝谢了,递给门徒,
说:"你们都拿这个喝;这杯是用我的血所立的新约,为你们和众人,
为赦罪流的。你们每次喝的时候,应该这样行,以记念我。"
我们同吃这饼,同饮这杯,
要宣扬祂的死。
我们如此行,直到祂再来。
主耶稣,我愿你来。
天父,我們追念圣子的受死和荣耀复活。
求你差遣圣灵,使我們更新,并与你圣子的身体联合,
得以与众圣徒,进入你永恒国度的喜乐,同享筵席,一起永远赞美说:
願一切赞美、尊貴、榮耀与权柄,都归与上帝被杀的羔羊,从現在直到永远,阿們。

THE BREAKING OF THE BREAD AND THE COMMUNION

19. **If the bread has not already been broken, the priest does so here. This may be done in silence, or the following may be said.**

    [We break this bread to share in the body of Christ.]

    We who are many are one body,

    for we all share in the one bread.

20. **Those who distribute the bread and deliver the cup may say**

    The body of our Lord Jesus Christ, which was given for you, preserve your body and soul to everlasting life. Take and eat this in remembrance that Christ died for you, and feed on him in your heart by faith with thanksgiving.

    The blood of our Lord Jesus Christ, which was shed for you, preserve your body and soul to everlasting life. Drink this in remembrance that Christ's blood was shed for you, and be thankful.

Or, the priest may say

Draw near with faith, to feed on Christ in your hearts with thanksgiving.

Those who distribute the bread and deliver the cup may say

The body of Christ keep you in eternal life. **Amen.**
The blood of Christ keep you in eternal life. **Amen.**

19. 牧师可在此时擘饼。

可安静地擘饼，也可说以下的话。

> 我們雖眾，仍屬一体，
> **因為我們都是分享這餅。**

20. 分发者可以说：

> 我们主耶稣基督的身体，为你而舍，保守你的身体和灵魂进入永生。你要以感恩和信心领受这饼，记念基督为你受死。
>
> 我们主耶稣基督的宝血，为你而流，保守你的身体和灵魂进入永生。你要以感恩的心领受这杯，记念基督为你流血。

或

牧师说：

> 以信心近前来，用感恩的心领受基督的身体和宝血。

其他分发者可说：

> 基督的身体，保守你进入永生。**阿们！**
> 基督的宝血，保守你进入永生。**阿们！**

THE SENDING OUT OF GOD'S PEOPLE

21. If the Lord's Prayer has not been said earlier (at 12), it is said here. This or another thanksgiving is then said.

> Gracious God, thank you for feeding us
> with the spiritual food of the body and blood
>   of our Saviour Jesus Christ.
> Thank you for assuring us of your goodness and love,
> and that we are living members of Christ's body.

22. All say together

> Father,
> **we offer ourselves to you**
> **as a living sacrifice**
> **through Jesus Christ our Lord.**
> **Send us out in the power of your Spirit**
> **to live and work to your praise and glory.**

23. This Hymn of Praise or a suitable alternative may be said or sung.

> **Glory to God in the highest,**
> **and peace to God's people on earth.**
> **Lord God, heavenly King,**
> **almighty God and Father,**
>   **we worship you, we give you thanks,**
>   **we praise you for your glory.**
> **Lord Jesus Christ, only Son of the Father,**
>   **Lord God, Lamb of God,**
>   **you take away the sin of the world:**
>   **have mercy on us;**
>   **you are seated at the right hand of the Father:**
>   **receive our prayer.**
> **For you alone are the Holy One,**
>   **you alone are the Lord,**
>   **you alone are the Most High**
>   **Jesus Christ,**
>   **with the Holy Spirit,**
>   **in the glory of God the Father. Amen.**

差遣

21. 如果之前没有宣读主祷文,现在可宣读。

可宣读以下,或其他的感恩祷文。

> 恩慈的上帝,感謝你以我們救主基督的聖體和寶血,作為靈糧喂養我們。使我們確实知道你的良善與慈愛,並且知道我們是屬基督身体的活潑肢体。

22. 会众同读:

> 天父,我们将自己当作活祭献上,
> 求主赐给我们力量和勇气,
> 专心乐意地敬爱主,服侍主;
> 奉我们主耶稣基督的名求。 阿们。

23. 诗歌

> 惟愿在上荣耀归于上帝,
> 在地有 平安,人都蒙恩。
> 我们赞美主、称颂主、
> 敬拜主、荣耀主;
> 为主的大荣耀,感谢主上帝、
> 天 上的王、全能的上帝圣父。
> 主独生圣子耶稣基督、
> 主上帝、上帝的羔羊,
> 除掉世上罪的主,怜悯我们;
> 坐在上帝圣父右边的主,
> 允准我们的祷告,
> 因为基督独一为圣,
> 基督独一为主,
> 基督独一与圣灵,在
> 上帝圣父荣 耀里为至上。阿们

24. The priest says this or an appropriate seasonal Blessing.

The peace of God which passes all understanding keep your hearts and minds in the knowledge and love of God, and of his Son, Jesus Christ our Lord;

and the blessing of God almighty, the Father, the Son, and the Holy Spirit, be among you and remain with you always. **Amen.**

25. The deacon may say

Go in peace to love and serve the Lord:

In the name of Christ. Amen.

24. 牧者用以下,或其他合适的祝文祝福

愿上帝所赐出人意外的平安,保守你们的心怀意念,使你们晓得敬爱上帝和他的圣子,我们的救主耶稣基督。又愿全能的上帝,圣父、圣子、圣灵,赐福给你们,直到永远。阿们。

25. 主礼说:

你们要平平安安地去敬爱主,服侍主。
奉基督的名。阿们。

HOLY BAPTISM CONFIRMATION IN HOLY COMMUNION

Together with provision for reaffirmation of baptismal vows and reception

When this service includes confirmation the presiding minister is the bishop.

GATHERING AND PREPARATION

1. A hymn, psalm or anthem may be sung.

2. The Greeting. The priest greets the people in these or other suitable words.

> The grace of the Lord Jesus Christ, and the love of God, and the fellowship of the Holy Spirit, be with you all.
>
> **And also with you.**

Or

> The Lord be with you.
>
> **And also with you.**

Or, from Easter Day to Pentecost

> Christ is risen. [Alleluia.]
>
> **He is risen indeed. [Alleluia.]**

3. A Sentence of Scripture appropriate to the day or the occasion may be read, or the following dialogue used.

> There is one Body and one Spirit;
>
> **there is one hope in God's call to us.**
>
> One Lord, one Faith, one Baptism,
>
> **one God and Father of all.**

4. The priest may continue with these or similar words here or after the sermon.

> Baptism is the gift of our Lord Jesus Christ.
>
> When he had risen from the dead, he commanded his followers to go and make disciples of all nations, baptising them in the name of the Father, and of the Son and of the Holy Spirit. We have come together today to obey that command. Baptism with water signifies the cleansing from sin that Jesus' death makes possible, and the new life that God gives us through the Holy Spirit. In baptism, the promises of God are visibly signed and sealed for us. We are joined to Christ, and made members of his body, the Church universal.

洗礼、坚信礼圣餐崇拜
包括确信礼和接纳礼

若此崇拜包括坚振礼，需要由主教主持。

宣召和预备

1. 诗歌

2. 问安（用以下，或其他合适的言语）
   主耶稣基督的恩惠、上帝的慈爱、圣灵的感动常與你們同在。
   也與你同在。

   或　主与你们同在。

   也與你同在。

   或　（从复活节到五旬节）

   基督已经复活。【哈利路亚】
   祂确实已经复活。【哈利路亚】

3. 当日宣召经文，或是以下回应

   只有一个身体，和一个圣灵；
   正如我们蒙召，有同一个指望。
   一主，一信，一洗，
   独一上帝，众人之父。

4. 主礼可在此宣读以下，或其他类似的句子，也可在讲道後宣读。

   洗礼是我们主耶稣基督所赐的礼物。当他从死里复活後，他命令门徒们去使万民他的门徒，奉父、子、圣灵的名为他们施洗。今天我们一同聚集，遵守这命令。洗礼的水，是表明藉着耶稣的死，洗净我们的罪，上帝透过圣灵赐给我们新生命。藉着洗礼，上帝彰显他的应许和印记。我们与基督联合，加入普世教会，成为他的身体。

[**When children are to be baptised, the priest says**

Children are baptised in response to God's all-embracing love. Parents and godparents who have responded to that love come now to bring their children for baptism. Before this congregation they must express their own trust and commitment to the promises of God, and their intention to bring up their children in the faith and practice of the Church. In due time these children should make their own response to God, and be prepared for confirmation.]

[**When there are candidates for confirmation, the bishop says**

In confirmation those who have been previously baptised come to confirm their baptismal promises and join with the other candidates to receive the laying on of the bishop's hand with prayer. We pray that those who are baptised and confirmed will be empowered by the Holy Spirit for the ministry and service to which God shall call them.]

So we welcome you, name(s), with your sponsors [and families].

We give thanks for you, and pray that you may know God's love and faithfulness for ever.

5. The priest says

Let us affirm our trust in God's mercy,
and confess that we need forgiveness.
[Let us pray.]

A pause for reflection

Lord God, you created this world, and made us in your own image. Forgive us when we turn away from you.
Lord, have mercy.
   Lord, have mercy.

Lord God, through your Son you overcame evil and death. Rescue us from slavery to sin.
   Christ, have mercy.
   Christ, have mercy.

若有儿童洗礼，主礼可说：

> 儿童的受洗，是父母和教父母为了要回应上帝的大爱。在会众面前，他们要向上帝的应许表达信任和承诺，以教会的信仰和实践来抚养孩子，直到他们长大後，通过坚信礼，自己向上帝回应。

若有 坚信礼，主教说：

> 坚信礼是为了那些曾经受洗，现在来重申信仰承诺，并接受主教按手祷告的人而设立。求主赐力量给这些受洗和接受坚信的人，使他们按着上帝的呼召来事奉和敬拜。
> 我们欢迎你，<u>名字</u>，和你的引荐人和家人。
> 我们为你献上感恩，并求主使你明白他永恒的慈爱和信实。

5. 主礼

> 让我们重申信靠上帝有怜悯，
> 并承认我们需要他的赦免。
> 让我们一起祷告…

片刻安静反省

> 主啊，你创造了这个世界，并照你的形象创造了我们。当我们背离你的时候，求你赦免我们。
> 求主怜悯。
> **求主怜悯。**
> 主上帝，你藉着你的儿子战胜了魔鬼和死亡。求你救我们脱离罪的奴役。
> 求基督怜悯。
> **求基督怜悯。**

Lord God, by your Spirit, you restore us to fellowship
with you and with one another. Breathe your love and freedom into our lives.

Lord, have mercy.

Lord, have mercy.

The priest says

Almighty God have mercy on you,

forgive you your sins,

and keep you in life eternal. **Amen.**

6. This Hymn of Praise or some other may be said or sung.

Glory to God in the highest,
and peace to God's people on earth.
Lord God, heavenly King,
almighty God and Father,
   we worship you, we give you thanks,
   we praise you for your glory.
Lord Jesus Christ, only Son of the Father,
   Lord God, Lamb of God,
   you take away the sin of the world:
      have mercy on us;
   you are seated at the right hand of the Father:
      receive our prayer.
For you alone are the Holy One:
you alone are the Lord:
you alone are the Most High,
   Jesus Christ,
   with the Holy Spirit,
   in the glory of God the Father. Amen.

7. The priest says

Let us pray.

The community may pray silently.

The priest then says or sings the Collect of the Day.

主上帝，藉着你的灵帮助我们恢复与你和他人的团契。在我们的生命中活出你的慈爱和自由。
求主怜悯。
求主怜悯。

牧师说：

全能的上帝怜悯你们，赦免你们的罪，并保守你们进入永生。**阿们。**

6. 诗歌

**惟愿在上荣耀归于上帝，
在地有 平安，人都蒙恩。
我们赞美主、称颂主、
敬拜主、荣耀主；
为主的大荣耀，感谢主上帝、
天 上的王、全能的上帝圣父。
主独生圣子耶稣基督、
主上帝、上帝的羔羊，
除掉世上罪的主，怜悯我们；
坐在上帝圣父右边的主，
允准我们的祷告，
因为基督独一为圣，
基督独一为主，
基督独一与圣灵，在
上帝圣父荣 耀里为至上。阿们**

7. 牧师说：

让我们一起祷告。

会众可在此无声祷告。

牧师最後读当日祷文。

THE MINISTRY OF THE WORD

8. The Reading(s) from the Old Testament and/or the New Testament as appointed.

After each reading the reader may say

> Hear the word of the Lord,
> **thanks be to God.**

Silence may follow each reading.

A psalm, hymn or anthem may be sung between the readings.

9. All stand for the Gospel Reading.

The deacon or other reader may say

> The Lord be with you.
> **And also with you.**

The reader says

> The Gospel of our Lord Jesus Christ according to…
> [chapter… verse…]
> **Glory to you Lord Jesus Christ.**

After the Gospel, the reader says

> This is the Gospel of the Lord,

Or

> [For] the Gospel of the Lord,
> praise to you Lord Jesus Christ.

10. The Sermon

Silence may follow.

圣言职事

8. 宣读圣经（旧约、新约）

每次读完，可用以下做回应

 聆听上帝的道。
  感谢上帝。

可加入诗歌

9. 宣读福音书（全体起立）

 主与你们同在。
  也与你同在。

宣读者宣读前当说：

 我们主耶稣基督的福音，是记载在____书，第____章，第____到第____节，
 荣耀归於主耶稣基督
 ……

福音书读毕後：

 这是主的福音，
 愿赞美归於主耶稣基督。

10. 讲道

THE PRESENTATION

11. The priest invites all candidates and their sponsors to stand in view of the congregation.

12. The priest invites the sponsors to present their baptismal candidates.

    We welcome those who come(s) to be baptised. I invite their sponsors to present them now.

    The sponsors answer

    We present name(s) **to be baptised**.

13. The priest says to the sponsors of those unable to answer for themselves

    Will you accept the responsibilities placed upon you in bringing name/this child for baptism?

    I will.

    Are you willing to answer on behalf of name/this child?

    I am.

    By your own prayers and example, by your friendship and love, will you encourage name/this child in the life and faith of the Christian community?

    I will, with God's help.

14. The bishop invites the sponsors of confirmation candidates to present the candidates.

    We welcome those who have come to be confirmed. I invite their sponsors to present them now.

    The sponsors answer

    We present name(s) **who come(s) to be confirmed.**

15. The bishop invites the sponsors of reaffirmation candidates to present the candidates.

    We welcome those who have been baptised and confirmed, and now come to seek God's blessing as they reaffirm their faith. I invite their sponsors to present them now.

    The sponsors answer

    We present name(s) **who come(s) to reaffirm** their **faith.**

11. 牧师邀请所有受洗者和他们的引荐人面对会众站立。

12. 牧师邀请引荐人介绍他们的受洗者。

    我们欢迎这些接受洗礼的人，我现在邀请他们的引荐人介绍他们。

引荐人回应

    我/我们引荐　姓名　领受洗礼。

13. 牧师对那些不能自己回答的引荐人说：

    你愿意接受因带领　儿童的名字　所要承担的责任吗？
    我愿意。
    你愿意代表　儿童的名字　回答问题吗？
    我愿意。
    你们是否愿意用自己的祷告和榜样、友谊和爱培育他们，在基督教的群体中成长？
    我愿意，求主帮助。

14. 主教邀请引荐人介绍接受坚信礼者。

    我们欢迎这些来接受坚信礼的人，现在邀请他们的引荐人来介绍他们。

引荐人回应

    我/我们引荐　姓名　接受坚振礼。

15. 主教邀请重申信仰的引荐人介绍他们。

    我们欢迎这些已经接受过洗礼和坚信礼的人，现在他们来寻求上帝的祝福，再次重申他们的信仰。我邀请他们的引荐人来介绍他们。

引荐人回应

    我/我们引荐　姓名　重申他们的信仰。

THE DECISION

16. The priest says to the candidates able to answer for themselves, and to the sponsors of other candidates

Before God and this congregation, you must affirm that you turn to Christ and reject all that is evil:

Do you turn to Christ?
I turn to Christ.
Do you repent of your sins?
I repent of my sins.
Do you reject selfish living, and all that is false and unjust?
I reject them all.
Do you renounce Satan and all evil?
I renounce all that is evil.

Almighty God deliver you from the powers of darkness, and lead you in the light of Christ to his everlasting kingdom. **Amen.**

17. The priest says to the candidates and sponsors

Will you each, by God's grace, strive to live as a disciple of Christ, loving God with your whole heart, and your neighbour as yourself, until your life's end?

I will, with God's help.

18. The priest says to the congregation

You have heard these our brothers and sisters respond to Christ. Will you support them in this calling?

The congregation answers

We will.

决定

16. 牧师向所有能自己回答的人，和孩童的引荐人说：

   在上帝和会众前，你（们）要确定回转归向基督，并且拒绝一切邪恶：
   你（们）要转向耶稣吗？
   我要转向耶稣。

   你（们）要悔改你（们）的罪吗？
   我要悔改我的罪。
   你（们）要弃绝自私的生活、一切的虚假和不义吗？
   我要弃绝这些。

   你（们）要弃绝拒绝撒旦和一切的邪恶吗？
   我要拒绝一切邪恶。

17. 牧师说：

   你（们）愿意靠上帝的恩典，一生尽力活出基督门徒的生命。全心全意敬爱上帝，并爱人如己吗？
   我愿意，求上帝帮助。

18. 牧师向会众说：

   你们见证了这些弟兄姐妹对基督呼召的回应。你们愿意支持他们吗？

会众回应

   我们愿意。

19. The priest says

> Let us pray.
>
> Grant, merciful God, that these persons may be so buried with Christ in baptism that the new nature may be raised up in them. May the fruit of your Spirit grow and flourish in them. **Amen.**
>
> Give to their sponsors [and their families] the desire to share with them what you have revealed in your holy gospel. **Amen.**
>
> [Give to those who come to affirm their baptism, strength and grace that they may faithfully serve you all their lives. **Amen.**]
>
> May they know Christ's forgiving love and continue in the fellowship and service of his Church. May they proclaim, by word and example, the good news of God in Christ. **Amen.**
>
> We thank you for the ministry we have in your world and to each other in the household of faith. Hasten that day when the whole creation shall be made perfect in Christ. **Amen.**

20. A hymn may be sung.

THE BAPTISM

21. The priest comes to the place where the water for baptism is, and begins the thanksgiving.

> [The Lord be with you.
> **And also with you.**]
> Let us give thanks to the Lord our God.
> **It is right to give our thanks and praise.**

The priest or other minister continues

> We give you thanks that at the beginning of creation your Holy Spirit moved upon the waters to bring forth light and life. With water you cleanse and replenish the earth; you nourish and sustain all living things.
> **Thanks be to God.**

19. 主礼说：

> 我们一起祷告：
> 仁慈的上帝，求你使他们藉着洗礼，与基督一同埋葬，并得到新的生命。愿你圣灵的果子在他们里面不断成长和茂盛。**阿们。**
>
> 愿他们的引荐人（或是家人）常与他们分享你所启示的福音真理。**阿们。**
> 【求你赐力量和恩典给那些重新确认自己信仰的人，使他们一生能忠心服侍你。**阿们。**】
> 愿他们明白基督宽恕的爱，并持续在教会中参与和服侍。让他们透过自己的言行，传扬基督的好消息。**阿们。**
> 我们感谢你让我们在天国的事奉中有份。愿一切被造之物在基督再来的日子得以完全。**阿们。**

20. 诗歌

    洗礼

21. 牧师站在洗礼位置

    > 愿主与你们同在。
    > **也与你同在。**
    > 感谢我主上帝。
    > **感谢和赞美他是应当的。**

牧师或主礼继续：

> 主，我们感谢你。因在创造之初，你的灵运行在水面上，带来了光和生命。你用水洁净和滋润大地，滋养和维持所有的生命。
> **感谢上帝。**

We give you thanks that through the waters of the Red Sea you led your people out of slavery into freedom, and brought them through the river Jordan to new life in the land of promise.

Thanks be to God.

We give you thanks for your Son Jesus Christ: for his baptism by John, for his anointing with the Holy Spirit.

Thanks be to God.

We give you thanks that through the deep waters of death Jesus delivered us from our sins and was raised to new life in triumph.

Thanks be to God.

We give you thanks for the grace of the Holy Spirit who forms us in the likeness of Christ and leads us to proclaim your kingdom.

Thanks be to God.

The priest continues

And now we give you thanks that you have called name/these your servants to new birth in your Church through the waters of baptism.

Pour out your Holy Spirit in blessing and sanctify this water so that those who are baptised in it may be made one with Christ in his death and resurrection. May they die to sin, rise to newness of life, and continue for ever in Jesus Christ our Lord, through whom we give you praise and honour in the unity of the Spirit, now and for ever. **Amen.**

22. The priest says to the candidates able to answer for themselves, and to the sponsors of other candidates

I now ask you to affirm as yours the faith of the Church.
Do you believe in God the Father?
I believe in God, the Father almighty,
　　creator of heaven and earth.

我们感谢你带领你的百姓经过红海的水，从奴役中得自由；又带领他们过约旦河，进入应许之地过新生活。
感谢上帝。
我们感谢你的圣子耶稣基督，接受施洗约翰的洗礼，并被圣灵膏抹。
感谢上帝。
我们感谢耶稣的受死，拯救我们脱离罪，并得到新的生命。
感谢上帝。
我们感谢圣灵的工作，使我们更像基督，并带领我们宣扬上帝的国度。
感谢上帝。

牧师继续

现在我们献上感恩，因为你呼召这些人（名字），使他们在教会藉着洗礼，得着新的生命。
愿圣灵赐福和洁净这水，使领受洗礼的人与基督同死，同复活。
使他们向罪死去，并复活成为一个全新的生命，永远活在我们主耶稣基督里。在圣灵里与耶稣基督联合，我们向你献上赞美和尊荣，从今直到永远。**阿们。**

22. 牧师向所有能自己回答的人，和孩童的引荐人说：

现在我要求你（们）确认自己对教会的信仰。
你是否相信圣父上帝？
我信上帝，
全能的父，
创造天地的主。

Do you believe in God the Son?

I believe in Jesus Christ, God's only Son, our Lord,
   who was conceived by the Holy Spirit,
   born of the virgin Mary,
   suffered under Pontius Pilate,
   was crucified, died, and was buried;
   he descended to the dead.
   On the third day he rose from the dead;
   he ascended into heaven,
   and is seated at the right hand of the Father;
   from there he will come to judge
   the living and the dead.

Do you believe in God the Holy Spirit?

I believe in the Holy Spirit,
   the holy catholic Church,
   the communion of saints,
   the forgiveness of sins,
   the resurrection of the body,
   and the life everlasting. Amen.

The priest says to the congregation

   This is the faith of the Church.

The congregation responds

   This is our faith:
   We believe in one God:
   Father, Son and Holy Spirit.

23. Each candidate is brought to the water.

The minister baptises by dipping the candidates in the water,
   or pouring water over them, saying
   Name, I baptise you in the name of the Father,
      and of the Son,
      and of the Holy Spirit.

And each one of them answers with their sponsors and the congregation
   Amen.

你是否相信圣子？
我相信我们的主耶稣基督，上帝的独生子，
因圣灵感孕，由童贞女玛利亚所生，
在本丢彼拉多手下受难，受死，埋葬，降在阴间，
第三天从死人中复活，升天，坐在全能父上帝的右边，
他将再临审判活人死人。
你是否相信圣灵？
我信圣而公之教会，
圣而公之教会，
我信圣徒相通，
我信罪得赦免，
我信身体复活，
我信永生。

阿们！

牧师向会众说

这是教会的信仰。

会众回应

这是我们的信仰：我们信独一真神，圣父、圣子、圣灵。

23. 进入洗礼

主礼洗礼时说

<u>姓名</u>，我奉圣父、圣子、圣灵的名为你施洗。

受礼者回应

阿们！

AFTER BAPTISM

24. When all have been baptised, the priest makes a cross on the forehead of each person, saying

> Name, I sign you with the sign of the cross to show that you are marked as Christ's own for ever.

The priest addresses all the newly baptised

> Live as a disciple of Christ:
> fight the good fight,
> finish the race,
> keep the faith.

And the congregation responds, saying

> **Confess Christ crucified,**
> **proclaim his resurrection,**
> **look for his coming in glory.**

25. *The minister says*

> God has brought you out of darkness
> into his marvellous light.

The congregation joins the minister saying

> **Shine as a light in the world**
> **to the glory of God the Father.**

26. *The minister continues*

> God has called you into his Church.

The congregation joins the minister in saying

> **We therefore receive and welcome you**
> **as a member with us of the body of Christ,**
> **as a child of the one heavenly Father,**
> **and as an inheritor of the kingdom of God.**

Where there is no confirmation, the service continues with the Greeting of Peace, ¶ 33.

洗礼後

24. 所有人受洗後，牧师在他们额上画十字记号

   <u>姓名</u>，我将十字圣号画在你的额上，表明你永远属於基督。

牧师向所有新受洗基督徒勉励

   以基督门徒的身份来生活，打美好的仗，完成当跑的路，持守所信的道。

会众回应：

   承认耶稣曾经受死，
   宣告耶稣已经复活，
   盼望祂荣耀的再临。

25. 主礼说：

   上帝已经带领你（们）出黑暗，进入他奇妙的光明中。

会众一起说：

   当作光照亮世界，
   把荣耀归给父上帝。

26. 主礼

   上帝呼召你（们）进入祂的教会。

会众同说：

   我们接纳并欢迎你（们）加入基督的身体，成为天父的儿女、天国的後嗣。

如果没有坚信礼，请跳至问安

CONFIRMATION

27. A hymn may be sung.

28. The bishop says

Our help is in the name of the Lord
who made heaven and earth.
Blessed be the name of the Lord
now, and for ever. Amen.

The bishop continues

Almighty and everliving God,
  you have given your servants
  new birth by water and the Spirit,
  and have forgiven them their sins.
Strengthen them, we pray, with the Holy Spirit
  that they may grow in grace.
Increase in them the spirit of wisdom
  and understanding,
  the spirit of discernment and inner strength,
  the spirit of knowledge and true godliness,
and fill them with wonder and awe at your presence,
through Jesus Christ our Lord. **Amen.**

29. Those who are to be confirmed kneel before the bishop, who lays a hand upon each of them saying

Strengthen, Lord, your servant, name with your Holy Spirit.
[Empower and sustain him/her for your service.]

And each of them answers with the congregation
  Amen.

The congregation joins the bishop in saying this prayer after all the candidates have received the laying on of hands, or the bishop alone may use this prayer instead of 'Strengthen, Lord…' when laying hands on each candidate.

Defend, O Lord, these your servants
with your heavenly grace,
that they may continue yours for ever,
and daily increase in your Holy Spirit more and more
until they come to your everlasting kingdom. Amen.

坚信礼

27. 诗歌

28. 主教说：

> 我们的帮助是来自主的名，
> **祂创造天地。**
> 主的名是应当称颂的，
> **从今时直到永远。阿们。**

主教继续

> 全能永生的上帝，你藉着水和圣灵，赐给你仆人们新生的生命，赦免了他们的罪。求圣灵赐力量给他们在恩典中成长。
> 增加他们智慧、聪明和分辨的能力，与内在的力量，并有知识和敬虔，使他们看见你的奇妙和伟大。
> 奉我们主耶稣基督的名求。**阿们。**

29. 所有接受坚信礼的人跪在主教前接受按手

> 求圣灵坚固你的仆人 姓名。

接受按手者回应

> **阿们。**

所有人接受按手後，会众和主教一同祷告

> **主啊！求你用属天的恩典，保守你的仆人们，使他们每日被圣灵更新，不断成长，直到进入你永恒的国度。**
> **阿们。**

REAFFIRMATION

30. Those receiving the laying on of hands for reaffirmation kneel before the bishop, who lays hands upon each saying

> Name, may the Holy Spirit
> who has begun a good work in you
> direct and uphold you
> in the service of Christ and his kingdom.
> God, the Father, the Son and the Holy Spirit,
> bless, preserve and keep you.

And each one of them answers with the congregation

> Amen.

RECEPTION

31. Baptised, communicant members of other churches who wish to be received into communicant membership of this church may be presented to the bishop according to the service of Reception into Communicant.

The candidate is presented by the priest and/or a lay sponsor.

> Name has already been baptised and has formerly been a communicant member of the ... Church. S/he now asks to be received into communicant membership of the Anglican Church of Australia and seeks our prayers in the fellowship of this parish.

The bishop says to the candidate

> Do you stand by the Christian confession and commitment made at your baptism?
>
> > I do.
>
> Do you desire to be admitted into communicant membership of the Anglican Church of Australia and accept her doctrine and order?
>
> > I do.

确信礼

30. 所有接受确信礼的人跪在主教面前接受按手

　　<u>姓名</u>，愿那位已经在你身上动工的圣灵，继续引导和保守你事奉基督和祂的国度。愿上帝，父圣、圣子、圣灵赐福、保守和坚固你。

接受按手者回应

　　阿们。

接纳礼

31. 已经在其他教会接受洗礼者，希望能加入此教会，可来到主教面前。主教说：

　　<u>姓名</u> 以前曾经受洗，是其他基督教会的会友，现在要求成为澳大利亚圣公会的会友，让我们为他们祷告。
　　你愿按照你受洗时所宣信的基督真理生活吗？
　　我愿意。
　　你愿意加入澳洲圣公会并且接受他的教义吗？
　　我愿意。

The bishop welcomes the person in these words, taking him/her by the hand.

We recognise you as a baptised and communicant member of the Christian Church.

The congregation responds

We receive and welcome you into the communion of the Anglican Church.

The bishop says

The Lord be with you.
And also with you.
Let us pray.
God of wisdom and love,
source of all good,
by your Holy Spirit strengthen your servant
and guide him/her in your way of peace and love.
We ask this through our Lord Jesus Christ your Son,
who lives and reigns with you
and the Holy Spirit,
one God, for ever and ever. **Amen.**

The candidate kneels and the bishop lays hands on the candidate's head, saying

Name, may the Holy Spirit direct and uphold you
in the service of Christ and his kingdom
in the fellowship of this Church.
God, the Father, the Son, and the Holy Spirit
bless, preserve and keep you.
Amen.

主教与转会的人握手并欢迎他们。

我们承认你已经受洗并成为基督教会的成员。

会众

我们接纳并欢迎你（们）进入圣公会教会。

主教

愿主与你们同在

也与你同在

让我们低头祷告，满有智慧和慈爱的上帝，众善的源头，藉你的圣灵加添你仆人的力量，并带领他们进入你的平安与大爱。奉与你一同掌权，我们主耶稣基督你的爱子，和圣父，圣灵的名求。**阿们。**

转会者跪在主教面前。

<u>姓名</u>　愿圣灵带领并赐你力量，在这个群体中服侍基督和他的国度。圣父，圣子和圣灵赐福，保守和坚固你。　**阿们。**

AFTER THE LAYING OF HANDS

32. The bishop prays for those upon whom hands have been laid.

>Almighty and everliving God,
>watch over these your servants
>>upon whom we have now laid our hands.
>Let your Holy Spirit always be with them
>and lead them to know and obey your word,
>>that they may serve you in this life,
>>and dwell with you in the life to come:
>through Jesus Christ our Lord. **Amen.**

THE GREETINGS OF PEACE

33. All stand. The Greeting of Peace is introduced with these or other suitable words.

>In baptism, God has made us one in Christ.
>>**His Spirit is with us.**

The priest says

>The peace of the Lord be always with you.
>>**And also with you.**

All may exchange a sign of peace.

A hymn may be sung.

34. The gifts of the people are brought to the Lord's Table. They may be presented in silence or a suitable prayer, such as follows, may be used.

>Blessed are you, Lord, God of all creation.
>Through your goodness we have these gifts to share.
>Accept and use our offerings for your glory
>and for the service of your kingdom.
>>**Blessed be God for ever.**

按手後

32. 主教为已接受按手者祷告。

   全能永生的上帝,愿你看顾你的仆人们。愿你的圣灵永远与他们同在。引领他们学习并遵行你的话语,使他们能终身服侍你,住在你的里面,直到永生。这都是靠着我们主耶稣基督。**阿门。**

问安

33. 全体起立,互祝平安

   在洗礼中,神使我们在基督里成为一体。
   祂的灵与我们同在。

牧师说:

   愿主的平安常与你们同在。
   也与你同在。

会众互祝平安

可同时唱诗歌

34. 奉献(可唱诗歌)

奉献後可用以下,或其他祷文。

   创造天地的主,你配得称颂。因着你的恩典,我们才有能力奉献。愿你悦纳我们所献上的,使用在你荣耀的国度中。
   上帝永远配得称颂。

THE GREAT THANKSGIVING

35. The priest takes the bread and wine for the communion, places them on the Lord's Table, and says the following or another authorised Prayer of Thanksgiving and Consecration.

[The Lord be with you.
   And also with you.]
Lift up your hearts.
   We lift them to the Lord.
Let us give thanks to the Lord our God.
   It is right to give our thanks and praise.
All glory and honour be yours always and everywhere,
   mighty Creator, everliving God.
We give you thanks and praise for our Saviour Jesus Christ,
   who by the power of your Spirit was born of Mary
   and lived as one of us.
By his death on the cross
   and rising to new life,
   he offered the one true sacrifice for sin
   and obtained an eternal deliverance for his people.
In baptism you have united us to him
   and brought us out of darkness into light.
      You pour your Spirit upon us, filling us with your gifts,
      and calling us to serve you as a royal priesthood.
Therefore with angels and archangels,
   and with all the company of heaven,
   we proclaim your great and glorious name,
   for ever praising you and saying:
Holy, holy, holy Lord, God of power and might,
Heaven and earth are full of your glory.
Hosanna in the highest.
[Blessed is he who comes in the name of the Lord.
Hosanna in the highest.]

大祝谢文

35. 预备圣餐的饼和酒。牧师用以下或其他授权礼文作感恩和祝圣祷告。

主与你们同在。
也与你同在。
你们心里当仰望主。
我们心里仰望主。
我们应当感谢我主上帝。
感谢我主上帝是应当的。

全能、永生、创造的上帝，荣耀与权能全都属你。

我们为着救主耶稣基督而感谢赞美你，由马利亚受圣灵感孕而生住在我们中间。
他在十字架上的受死和复活，献上永远的赎罪祭，使属祂的人都得到永恒的救赎。

藉着洗礼，你使我们与基督联合，带我们脱离黑暗，进入光明。
你赐下圣灵，给我们各种恩赐，并呼召我们像尊贵的祭司一样服侍你。
因此，我们和天使并天使长，天上的会众，一同称赞颂扬主有荣耀的圣名，常赞美主说：
圣哉、圣哉、圣哉，天地万军的主上帝，
你的荣光充满天地。
奉主名而来的，当受赞美！
在至高之处，亦当称颂主！

Merciful God, we thank you
> for these gifts of your creation,
> this bread and wine,
> and we pray that by your Word and Holy Spirit,
> we who eat and drink them
> may be partakers of Christ's body and blood.

On the night he was betrayed Jesus took bread;
> and when he had given you thanks
> he broke it, and gave it to his disciples, saying,
> 'Take, eat. This is my body given for you.
> Do this in remembrance of me.'

After supper, he took the cup,
> and again giving you thanks
> he gave it to his disciples, saying,
> 'Drink from this, all of you.
> This is my blood of the new covenant
> shed for you and for many
> for the forgiveness of sins.
> Do this, as often as you drink it, in remembrance of me.'

The memorial acclamation is used here or below.

> **Christ has died.**
> **Christ is risen.**
> **Christ will come again.**

Therefore we do as our Saviour has commanded:
> proclaiming his offering of himself
> made once for all upon the cross,
> his mighty resurrection and glorious ascension,
> and looking for his coming again,
> we celebrate, with this bread and this cup,
> his one perfect and sufficient sacrifice
> for the sins of the whole world.

The memorial acclamation may be used here.

慈悲的上帝，我们因着这饼和杯感谢你。
我们向你祷告，藉着你的道和圣灵的力量，当我们领受这饼和杯时，就能同享基督的身体和宝血。

主耶稣被卖的那一夜，
拿起饼来，祝谢了，就掰开，分给他的门徒，
说："你们拿这个吃，这是我的身体，
是为你们舍的；你们应该这样行，以记念我。"
饭后，他也照样拿起杯来，祝谢了，递给门徒，
说："你们都拿这个喝；
这杯是用我的血所立的新约，
为你们和众人，为赦罪流的。
你们每次喝的时候，应该这样做，以记念我。"
基督曾经受死。
基督现已复活。
基督将要再临。
因此，我们按着主的命令：
宣扬祂在十字架上，为所有的人，把自己献上，
祂已复活，并荣耀地升天，
我们期待祂的再来。
我们以这饼和杯，感谢祂为全世界的罪，一次献上完美和足够的献祭。

Renew us by your Holy Spirit
  unite us in the body of your Son,
  and bring us with all your people
  into the joy of your eternal kingdom;
  through Jesus Christ our Lord,
  with whom, and in whom,
  in the fellowship of the Holy Spirit,
  we worship you, Father,
  in songs of never-ending praise:
  Blessing and honour and glory and power
  are yours for ever and ever. Amen.

36. The Lord's Prayer is said here or after the communion. The priest says

As our Saviour Christ has taught us, we are confident to pray,

Our Father in heaven,
  hallowed be your name,
  your kingdom come,
  your will be done,
  on earth as in heaven.
Give us today our daily bread.
Forgive us our sins
  as we forgive those who sin against us.
Save us from the time of trial
  and deliver us from evil.
For the kingdom, the power, and the glory are yours
now and for ever. Amen.

求圣灵更新我们，使我们与你的圣子合一，
带领我们和你的子民一同进入你永恒喜乐的国度；
奉我们主耶稣基督的名，并在圣灵的团契中，我们敬拜你，永远歌颂赞美你：
颂赞、尊贵、荣耀、权柄全是你的，直到永远。阿们。

36. 可在此，或圣餐後读主祷文：

    我们的救主耶稣基督曾教导我们这样祷告：
    我们在天上的父，
    愿人都尊你的名为圣。
    愿你的国降临。
    愿你的旨意行在地上，
    如同行在天上。
    我们日用的饮食，今日赐给我们。
    饶恕我们的罪，如同我们饶恕得罪我们的人。
    不叫我们遇见试探，救我们脱离凶恶。
    因为国度、权柄、荣耀、全是你的，
    直到永远，阿们。

THE BREAKING OF THE BREAD AND COMMUNION

37. The priest breaks the bread. One of the following may be said.

[We break this bread to share in the body of Christ.]
We who are many are one body,
for we all share in the one bread.

Or

As this broken bread was once many grains,
which have been gathered together and made one bread:
**so may your Church be gathered
from the ends of the earth into your kingdom.**

38. The priest and other communicants receive the Holy Communion.

The sacrament is given with the following words.

The body of our Lord Jesus Christ, which was given for you, preserve your body and soul to everlasting life. Take and eat this in remembrance that Christ died for you, and feed on him in your heart by faith with thanksgiving.

And

The blood of our Lord Jesus Christ, which was shed for you, preserve your body and soul to everlasting life. Drink this in remembrance that Christ's blood was shed for you, and be thankful.

Or, the priest says

[The gifts of God for the people of God.]

Come let us take this holy sacrament of the body and blood of Christ in remembrance that he died for us, and feed on him in our hearts by faith with thanksgiving.

The sacrament is given with the following words, after which the communicant responds, Amen.

The body of Christ [the bread of heaven] keep you in eternal life. **Amen.**
The blood of Christ [the cup of salvation] keep you in eternal life. **Amen.**

37. 牧师在此擘饼,并读以下其中一段。

我們虽众,仍属一体,
因为我們都是分享這餅。

或

这擘开的饼本是很多麦子,在一起成为了这饼:
愿你的教会从地极一同聚集,进入你的国度。

38. 分发圣餐

分发者可说:
我们主耶稣基督的身体,为你而舍,保守你的身体和灵魂进入永生。
以感恩和信心领受这饼,记念基督为你受死。

和

我们主耶稣基督的宝血,为你而流,保守你的身体和灵魂进入永生。
以感恩的心领受这杯,记念基督为你流血。

或

牧师说:
前来领受这圣礼,以记念耶稣基督为我们而死。以信心和感恩的心前来领受。

分发时可说:

基督的身体(天上的粮),保守你进入永生。**阿们!**
基督的宝血(救恩的杯),保守你进入永生。**阿们!**

During the communion, psalms, hymns and anthems such as those on page 145 may be sung or said.

THE SENDING OUT OF GOD'S PEOPLE

39. The priest says

>Let us pray.
>Gracious God,
>in baptism you make us one family in Christ your Son,
>one in the sharing of his body and his blood,
>one in the communion of his Spirit.
>Help us to grow in love for one another
>and come to the full maturity of the body of Christ.

40. All say together

>Father,
>**we offer ourselves to you**
>**as a living sacrifice**
>**through Jesus Christ our Lord.**
>**Send us out in the power of your Spirit**
>**to live and work to your praise and glory.**

Or

>Most loving God,
>**you send us into the world you love.**
>**Give us grace to go thankfully and with courage**
>**in the power of your Spirit.**

41. A hymn may be sung.

领受圣餐时唱诗歌或颂读诗篇。

差遣

39. 牧师说:

> 让我们一同祷告:
> 恩慈的上帝,
> 藉着洗礼,你使我们在基督里成为一家人,
> 一起分享祂的身体和宝血,
> 在祂的灵里合而为一。
> 帮助我们懂得彼此相爱,
> 并在基督的身体中不断成长。

40. 全体说:

> 天父,
> **我们奉我们主耶稣基督的名,把自己当作活祭献上。**
> **差遣我们带着圣灵的能力出去,在生活和工作上,把赞美和荣耀都归给你。**

或

> 最慈爱的上帝,
> **差遣我们出去你所爱的世界中。赐给我们圣灵的力量,带着感恩和信心出去。**

41. 诗歌

42. If there has been confirmation the bishop may say to the congregation

All who have been baptised and confirmed are called to study the Bible, to take part in the life of the Church, to share in the Holy Communion, and to pray faithfully and regularly.

We are called to share with others, by word and example, the love of Christ and his gospel of reconciliation and hope.

We are called to love our neighbours as ourselves, to honour all people and to pray and work for peace and justice.

I invite all of you to commit yourselves anew to this calling.

**We will gladly do so,
in the strength of the Holy Spirit.**

43. The priest or bishop blesses the congregation with this or another appropriate blessing.

Go forth into the world in peace;
be of good courage;
hold fast that which is good;
render to no one evil for evil;
strengthen the faint hearted; support the weak;
help the afflicted;
give honour to all; love and serve the Lord,
rejoicing in the power of the Holy Spirit;
and the blessing of God almighty,
the Father, the Son and the Holy Spirit,
be among you and remain with you always. **Amen.**

44. The deacon may say

Go in peace to love and serve the Lord:

In the name of Christ. Amen.

Or

Go in the name of Christ:

Thanks be to God.

42. 如果有坚振礼，主教向会众说：

所有受洗及接受坚振礼的人，是被呼召要学习圣经，参与教会生活，分享圣餐，并恒长专心祷告。
我们被呼召要在言语和行为上，与别人分享基督福音所带来的和好和盼望。
我们被呼召要爱人如己，敬重所有的人，并为和平和公义努力和祷告。
我邀请你们重新承诺这呼召。

我们乐意遵行，求圣灵帮助。

43. 牧师或主教祝福

平安的进入这个世界。
满怀信心，
持守良善，
不以恶报恶，
扶植软弱的人。
帮助在痛苦中的人，
敬重所有的人，敬爱主，服侍主，
在圣灵的大能中喜乐。
全能的上帝，圣父、圣子、圣灵赐福你们，常与你们同在，直到永远。
阿们。

44. 会吏说：

你们要平平安安的去敬爱主，服侍主。
奉耶稣基督的名。阿们。

或

奉基督的名出去。
感谢上主。

A SERVICE FOR MARRIAGE SECOND ORDER

GATHERING IN GOD'S NAME

1. The people stand as the wedding party takes its place.

    The couple, with the wedding party, stand before the minister in the presence of witnesses.

    The man may receive the woman's hand from a member of the family or a friend and similarly, the woman may receive the man's hand.

2. The minister may welcome the congregation as is appropriate to the occasion. The following greeting may be used.

    The grace of the Lord Jesus Christ,
    and the love of God,
    and the fellowship of the Holy Spirit
    be with you all.
    > **And also with you.**

3. This, or another appropriate Sentence of Scripture, may be read.

    God is love, and those who live in love live in God, and God lives in them.

    1 John 4.16.

4. A hymn or song may be sung.

5. The minister says

    We have come together in the presence of God
    to witness the marriage of N and N,
    and to ask God's blessing on them
    > as we share their joy.
    Marriage is a gift of God our creator.
    It is a symbol of God's unending love for his people,
    > and of the union between Christ and his Church.
    Christ loved his bride the Church,
    > and gave himself for her.
    As he has called N and N to marriage,
    so he draws their differing gifts and hopes
    into a unity of love and service.

婚礼
程序二

奉上帝的名聚集

1. 当新娘到场，所有人站立。

    新人站在主礼面前，新郎从新娘家人接新娘的手。

2. 主礼欢迎会众。

    愿主耶稣基督的恩惠，上帝的慈爱，和圣灵的感动交通，与你们同在。
    也与你同在。

3. 可读以下，或其他合适的经文。

    上帝就是爱，住在爱裏面的就是住在上帝裏面；上帝也住在他裏面。(约壹4:16)

4. 诗歌

5. 主礼
    我们一起来到上帝的面前，见证 姓名 先生和 姓名 女士的结婚典礼。
    我们在喜乐中，求上帝祝福他们，也让我们分享他们的喜乐。
    婚姻是上帝所赐的礼物，是上帝对祂子民永无止息的爱的象征，也是基督与他的教会联合的象征，基督爱他的教会，为教会舍己。
    当主呼召 姓名 和 姓名 进入婚姻，同时也把他们不同的恩赐和盼望，在爱和服事中合而为一。

Scripture teaches that marriage is a lifelong partnership
uniting a woman and a man in heart, mind and body.
In the joy of their union, husband and wife
    enrich and respond to each other,
growing in tenderness and understanding.
Through marriage a new family is formed,
where children may be born
and grow in secure and loving care.
Marriage is therefore to be honoured by all.
No one should enter it lightly or selfishly,
but responsibly and joyfully,
with mutual respect and the promise to be faithful.

So let us pray with N and N
as they prepare to exchange their solemn vows:

Blessed are you, loving God,
your Spirit binds us together.
    Crown our lives with your goodness;
    sustain us all our days with your love.
Bless N and N with wisdom and pleasure.
Be their friend and companion in joy,
their comfort in need and in sorrow.
And when this life is ended
welcome them into your presence,
there with all your people
to praise your holy name:
    Blessed be God; Father, Son and Holy Spirit,
    as in the beginning, so now, and for ever. Amen.

圣经教导我们，婚姻是一生之久的关系，是一个女人和一个男人在心灵、思想和身体上的结合。

在喜乐中结合，丈夫和妻子互相呼应并丰富对方，在温柔和理解中不断成长。

在婚姻中，一个新的家庭被建立，孩童也可以在一个安全和爱的环境下出生和成长。

因此，人人当尊重婚姻。

人不应当以轻率或自私的态度，而应当以真诚和喜乐的心态看待婚姻，互相尊重，和信守誓约。

所以，当 姓名 和 姓名 准备互相许下庄严的誓约时，我们为他们祷告：

我们赞美你，慈爱的上帝，

你的灵使我们联合在一起。

以你的良善作我们的冠冕，

以你的爱扶持我们的年日。

赐 姓名 和 姓名 智慧和欢乐。

在他们的喜乐中，像朋友一样陪伴他们，

在他们痛苦和需要时，安慰他们。

当生命终结时，迎接他们到你面前，与你的子民一起，赞美你的圣名：

赞美归於上帝，圣父、圣子、圣灵，

起初这样，现在这样，以後也这样，直到永远。阿们！

THE MINISTRY OF THE WORD

6. One or more Readings from the Scriptures. When the Holy Communion is to follow, there are at least two readings of which the final one is the Gospel.

After each reading the reader may say

> Hear the word of the Lord,
>
> **thanks be to God.**

A psalm, canticle, hymn, anthem or period of silence may follow the readings. When the Gospel is read, the congregation stands and the reading is preceded by these words

> The gospel of our Lord Jesus Christ according to ...

And there may be said

> **Glory to you, Lord Jesus Christ.**

After the Gospel the reader may say

> This is the Gospel of the Lord,

Or

> [For] the Gospel of the Lord,
>
> **praise to you, Lord Jesus Christ.**

7. An address appropriate to the occasion is delivered.

8. A hymn or song and other readings consistent with Christian teaching and the theme of the service may also be used.

圣言职事

6. 读经（若有圣餐，最少要读两处经文，而最後一处是福音书。）

读经後回应

> 聆听主的道。
> **感谢上帝。**

在读经後可有诗歌、宣读诗篇或安静。
宣读福音书时，会众起立，并按以下程序：

> 我们主耶稣基督的福音，是记载在…

会众一同说：

> 荣耀归於你，主耶稣基督。

宣读福音书後，读经者说：

> 这是主的福音。

或

> 主的福音。
> **赞美归於你，主耶稣基督。**

7. 劝勉

8. 诗歌或其他有关基督教的教导。

THE WEDDING

9. **The couple stand before the minister.**
   The minister says to the man

   > N, will you give yourself to N, to be her husband,
   > to live with her according to God's word?
   > Will you love her, comfort her,
   > honour and protect her,
   > and, forsaking all others, be faithful to her
   > so long as you both shall live?

   The man answers

   > **I will.**

   The minister says to the woman

   > N, will you give yourself to N, to be his wife,
   > to live with him according to God's word?
   > Will you love him, comfort him,
   > honour and protect him,
   > and, forsaking all others, be faithful to him
   > so long as you both shall live?

   The woman answers

   > **I will.**

10. **The minister says to the congregation**

    > Families and friends,
    > you are witnesses to these vows.
    > Will you do everything in your power
    > to uphold N and N in their marriage?
    > > **We will.**

婚礼

9. 新人在主礼面前站立

主礼对男方说：

　　姓名，你愿意娶 姓名 成为她的丈夫，
　　并按照上帝的道和她在一起生活吗？
　　你愿意一生爱她、安慰她、尊重她，保护她，并忠於她，胜过一切吗？

男方：

　　我愿意！

主礼对女方说：

　　姓名，你愿意嫁给 姓名 为妻，
　　并按照上帝的道 和他在一起生活吗？
　　你愿意一生爱他、安慰他、尊重他，保护他，并忠於他，胜过一切吗？

女方：

　　我愿意！

10. 主礼向会众说：

　　众亲友，你们是这对新人誓约的见证者。
　　你们愿尽一切所能支持 姓名 和 姓名 的婚姻吗？
　　我们愿意。

11. **The man, facing the woman and taking her hand in his, says**

> I, N, in the presence of God,
> take you, N, to be my wife:
> to have and to hold
> from this day forward,
> for better, for worse,
> for richer, for poorer,
> in sickness and in health,
> to love and to cherish,
> so long as we both shall live.
> All this I vow and promise.

They loose their hands.

The woman, still facing the man and taking his hand in hers, says

> I, N, in the presence of God,
> take you, N, to be my husband;
> to have and to hold
> from this day forward,
> for better, for worse,
> for richer, for poorer,
> in sickness and in health,
> to love and to cherish,
> so long as we both shall live.
> All this I vow and promise.

12. **When rings are to be given, the minister may receive them and may say**

> God of steadfast love,
> by your blessing,
> let these rings be for N and N
> a symbol of their love and faithfulness
> through Jesus Christ our Lord. **Amen.**

13. **The giver places the ring on the ring-finger of the other's hand and says**

> I give you this ring
> as a symbol of our marriage.
> With all that I am and all that I have
> I honour you; in the name of God. **Amen.**

11. 男方面对女方，握着她的手说：

我，姓名 在上帝面前，
迎娶你，姓名，成为我的妻子，
从今往后，在我们有生之年，
不论是顺境，还是逆境，
是富有，还是贫穷，
是病痛，还是健康，
我都爱你，珍惜你，
这是我的誓言和承诺！

松开手

女方面对男方，握着他的手说：

我，姓名 在上帝面前，
嫁给你，姓名，为妻，
从今往后，在我们有生之年，
不论在顺境，还是逆境，
是富有，还是贫穷，
是病痛，还是健康，
我都爱你，珍惜你，
这是我的誓言和承诺！

12. 主礼接过婚戒，说：

慈爱的上帝，求你赐福这两枚戒指，愿这两枚戒指成为 姓名 和 姓名 立志彼此相爱，彼此忠诚的象征。
奉我们主耶稣基督的名。**阿们！**

13. 新人给对方戴上戒指，说：

这是我与你结婚的戒指，是我们婚姻的信物。
奉上帝之名，我将以我所有的一切，一生来敬重你。**阿们！**

After rings have been exchanged, the man and woman may say together

> I receive this ring
> as a symbol of your love and faithfulness
> to the end of our days.

And/or

> May God enable us to grow in love together.

14. The minister joins their hands and declares to the people

> Before God and in the presence of us all,
> N and N have joined hands
> and made their solemn vows,
> promising life-long faithfulness to each other.
> In the name of God,
> I declare them to be husband and wife.
> What God has joined together,
> let no one separate.

The couple may say

> God of tenderness and strength,
> you have brought our paths together
> and led us to this day;
> go with us now as we travel through good times,
> through trouble, and through change.
> Bless our home, our partings and our meetings.
> Make us worthy of one another's best,
> and tender with one another's dreams. **Amen.**

15. The minister adds a blessing for the couple.

> God the Father lovingly enfold you,
> God the Son grace your home and table,
> God the Holy Spirit crown you with joy and peace.
> The Lord bless you and keep you in eternal life. **Amen.**

16. The marriage certificates are signed here or at the conclusion of the service.

交换婚戒後，新人一同说：

> 我接受这枚戒指，
> 作为你爱情和忠诚的信物，直至终生。

或／和

> 愿上帝使我们在爱里一起成长。

14. 主礼使新人的手握在一起，宣告：

> 在上帝和我们众人面前，姓名 和　姓名 手握手庄严誓言，承诺一生忠於对方。
> 我奉上帝的名，宣布他们为夫妻。
> 上帝结合的，人不得分开。

新人可说：

> 满有温柔和力量的上帝，
> 你使我们走在一起，并带领我们到　今天；不论我们将来要经历喜乐、困难或变迁，求你与我们同在。
> 不论我们在一起和不在一起的时候，都祝福我们的家庭。使我们成为对方最宝贵的人，彼此敬重关爱。**阿们。**

15. 主礼祝福新人

> 天父上帝用慈爱拥抱你们，
> 圣子上帝赐恩给你们的家庭，
> 圣灵上帝保守你们喜乐和平安。
> 愿主祝福你们，保守你们进入永生。**阿们。**

16. 婚书可在此，或婚礼最後签署。

THE PRAYERS OF THE PEOPLE

17. A selection of the following or other prayers is said. When the Holy Communion follows, A prayer for all people on page 172 is used here.

The prayers may be led by a friend or member of the families of the couple.

a For faithfulness
God of all grace,
friend and companion,
look in favour on N and N,
and all who are made one in marriage.
In your love deepen their love,
strengthen their wills
   to keep the promises they have made,
that they may continue
   in life-long faithfulness to each other;
through Jesus Christ our Lord. **Amen.**

b For the joy of loving
God our Creator,
we thank you for your gift of sexual love
by which husband and wife
   may delight in each other,
   and share with you the joy of creating new life.
By your grace may N and N remain lovers,
rejoicing in your goodness all their days. **Amen.**

c For children
Lord of life,
you shape us in your image,
and by your gracious gift
the human family is increased.
To N and N grant the blessing of children.
Fill them with wisdom and love
as they care for their family,
so that they and their children
may know and love you,
through your Son Jesus Christ our Lord. **Amen.**

祷告

17. 祷告
若有圣餐，用以下祷文。

祷告可由亲友带领。

a 为忠诚
恩典的上帝，
他们是朋友和伴侣，
愿你看顾 姓名 和 姓名 ，
和所有在婚姻中成为一体的人。
在你的爱中使他们的爱成长，
坚固他们的意志，
使他们能持守所做的承诺，
一生彼此忠于对方；
奉我们的主耶稣基督， **阿门！**

b 为爱中的喜乐
上帝，我们的创造者，
我们感谢你赐下性爱作礼物，
让丈夫和妻子能彼此欢愉，并与你分享创造新生命的喜乐。
在你的恩典中，让 姓名 和 姓名 继续相爱，一生在你的美善中享受喜乐。**阿门！**

c 為兒女
生命之主，
你按你自己的形象塑造了我們，
因着你的宝贵的礼物，家庭得以建立。
赐予 姓名 和 姓名 儿女的福乐。
在他们照顾家庭时，以爱与智慧充满他们，
使他们与他们的孩子能认识你，敬爱你，
奉圣子我们的主耶稣基督。**阿门！**

d For an existing family

God of all grace and goodness,
we thank you for this new family,
and for everything parents and children have to share;
by your Spirit of peace draw them together
and help them to be true friends to one another.
Let your love surround them
and your care protect them,
through Jesus Christ our Lord. **Amen.**

e For grace to live well

Faithful God,
giver of all good things,
give N and N wisdom and devotion
in the ordering of their life together.
May they dwell together in love and peace
all the days of their life,
    seeking one another's welfare,
    bearing one another's burdens,
    and sharing one another's joys;
through Jesus Christ our Lord. **Amen.**

f For discipleship

Eternal God,
without your grace nothing is strong, nothing is sure.
Strengthen N and N with patience, kindness, gentleness,
and all other gifts of the Holy Spirit,
so that they may fulfil the vows they have made.
Keep them faithful to each other and to you.
Fill them with such love and joy
that they may build a home of peace and welcome.
Make their life together a sign of Christ's love
    in this broken world,
that unity may overcome estrangement,
forgiveness heal guilt,
and joy conquer despair;
through Jesus Christ our Lord. **Amen.**

d 为家庭

恩典和美善的上帝,
我们为这新家庭,为父母与孩子所能分享的一切感谢你;
愿平安之灵使他们聚在一起,
帮助他们彼此成为真正的朋友。
让你的爱环绕他们, 你的关怀保护他们,
奉我们的主耶稣基督。**阿门!**

e 为恩典和美好的生活

信实的上帝,
赐一切美好事物的主,
在他们生活的规律中,
赐 姓名 和 姓名 智慧和忠诚。
愿他们在有生之年以爱与和平相处,
寻求彼此的福乐,
承担彼此的重担,
并分享彼此的喜乐;
奉我们的主耶稣基督。**阿门!**

f 为成为门徒

永恒的上帝,
没有你的恩典,就没有强壮,也没有肯定。
求你以忍耐,恩慈,温柔及其他圣灵的果子坚固 姓名 和 姓名,
使他们可以落实他们彼此的誓言。
保守他们彼此忠诚和对你忠诚。
让他们以爱和喜乐建立一个和平和好客的家。
让他们的生命能够在破碎的世界中见证基督的爱,
以合一战胜隔阂,
以宽恕医治罪疚,
以喜乐战胜绝望;
奉我们的主耶稣基督。**阿门!**

g For the families of the couple

Gracious Lord,

bless the parents and families of N and N

that they may grow in love and friendship.

Grant that, as they have witnessed these vows today,

they may find their lives enriched and strengthened

and their loyalties confirmed. **Amen.**

h For the healing of memory

Loving God,

you are merciful and forgiving.

Grant that those who are suffering the hurts of the past

   may experience your generous love.

Heal their memories, comfort them,

and send them all from here

renewed and hopeful. **Amen.**

i For the joy of companionship

All praise and blessing to you, God of love,

creator of the universe,

maker of man and woman in your likeness,

source of blessing for married life.

All praise to you, for you have created

   courtship and marriage,

     joy and gladness,

     feasting and laughter,

     pleasure and delight.

May your blessing come in full upon N and N.

May they know your presence

in their joys and in their sorrows.

May they reach old age in the company of friends

and come at last to your eternal kingdom. **Amen.**

g 为夫妇的家人

亲爱的主,
祝福 姓名 和 姓名 的父母与家人,
让他们的爱与友谊与日俱增。
今天他们见证了这些的誓言
愿他们的家庭得以滋润和坚固,
忠诚得到落实。

阿门!

h 医治记忆

慈爱的主,
你是怜悯和饶恕。
愿那些受苦和受伤人能经历你的大爱。
求你医治他们的记忆,安慰他们,
让他们更新,并充满希望地在这里踏上旅程 。**阿门!**

i 为相伴的喜乐

愿颂赞和祝福都归于你,慈爱的上帝,
宇宙的创造者,
你按你的形象造男,造女,
你是祝福婚姻的泉源。
愿颂赞归于你,因为你创造了爱情与婚姻,
喜乐与欢愉,
宴乐与笑声,
享乐与情趣。
愿你的祝福满满地临到 姓名 和 姓名。
愿他们在喜乐和悲伤中都感到你的同在。
愿他们在朋友的陪伴下,进入你永恒的国度。**阿门!**

Or

j A prayer for all people
Almighty God, look graciously on the world which you have made and for which your Son gave his life. Bless all whom you make one flesh in marriage. May their life together be a sign of your love to this broken world, so that unity may overcome estrangement, forgiveness heal guilt, and joy overcome despair.
Lord, in your mercy
hear our prayer.
May N and N so live together that the strength of their love may reflect your love and enrich our common life.
Lord, in your mercy
hear our prayer.
May they be gentle and patient, ready to trust each other, and, when they fail, willing to recognise and acknowledge their fault and to ask each other's forgiveness.
Lord, in your mercy
hear our prayer.
[May N and N be blessed with the gift of children. Fill them with wisdom and love as they care for their family.
Lord, in your mercy
hear our prayer.]
May the lonely, the bereaved, and all who suffer want or anxiety, be defended by you, O Lord.
Lord, in your mercy
hear our prayer.
May those whose lives are today brought together be given wisdom, patience and courage to serve one another in Christ's name.
Lord, in your mercy
hear our prayer.
May friends and family gathered here, and those separated by distance, be strengthened and blessed this day.
Lord, in your mercy
hear our prayer.
We praise you, merciful God, for those who have died in the faith of Christ. May we be strengthened by their example.

或

j 为众人祷告

全能的上帝，你的爱子为这世界舍弃了生命，因为你爱你所创造的世界。求你赐福所有你使他们在婚姻中结合的人。在这破碎世界里，让他们的生命成为你爱的标记，使合一战胜隔阂，原谅医治罪疚，喜乐战胜绝望。

主啊，求你怜悯。

垂听我们的祷告。

愿 姓名 和 姓名 的爱，能反映你自己的爱，使我们的生命更丰盛。

主啊，求你怜悯。

垂听我们的祷告。

愿他们以温柔和耐心相待，彼此信任；犯错时，勇于认错，并寻求原谅。

主啊，求你怜悯。

垂听我们的祷告。

【愿主赐孩子给 姓名 和 姓名 赐他们智慧和爱心管理他们的家。

主啊，求你怜悯。

垂听我们的祷告。】

主啊，愿你保护那些孤单，失去亲人，和生活在焦虑中的人。

主啊，求你怜悯。

垂听我们的祷告。

愿你赐智慧、忍耐和勇气给今天在这里相聚的人，能奉主的名互相服侍。

主啊，求你怜悯。

垂听我们的祷告。

愿你赐力量和恩福给每一位出席或缺席的亲戚朋友。主啊，求你怜悯。

垂听我们的祷告。

我们为那些去世了的信徒赞美你。愿他们的榜样成为我们的力量。

The prayers conclude with either

Almighty God, you have promised to hear our prayers.
Grant that what we have asked in faith
we may by your grace receive,
through Jesus Christ our Lord. Amen.

Or, unless the Lord's Prayer is said at ¶ 24

Accept our prayers, loving God, through Jesus Christ our Lord, who taught us to pray,
Our Father in heaven,
   hallowed be your name,
   your kingdom come,
   your will be done,
   on earth as in heaven.
Give us today our daily bread.
Forgive us our sins
   as we forgive those who sin against us.
Save us from the time of trial
   and deliver us from evil.
For the kingdom, the power, and the glory are yours
now and for ever. Amen.

以下其中一段作祷告结束

全能的上帝，你应许垂听我们的祷告。
求你因着你的恩典，赐我们凭信心所求的。奉我们主基督的名求。阿们。

或，除非之前已颂读过主祷文

爱我们的上帝，悦纳我们的祷告。我们主耶稣基督曾经教导我们祷告说：
**我们在天上的父，
愿人都尊你的名为圣。
愿你的国降临。
愿你的旨意行在地上，
如同行在天上。
我们日用的饮食，今日赐给我们。
饶恕我们的罪，如同我们饶恕得罪我们的人。
不叫我们遇见试探，救我们脱离凶恶。
因为国度、权柄、荣耀，全是你的，
直到永远，阿们。**

18. Unless the Holy Communion follows, the service concludes here with the blessing and dismissal. If the marriage certificates have not been signed, they are signed here.

May the God of steadfastness and encouragement
grant you to live in such harmony with one another,
in accord with Christ Jesus,
that together you may with one voice
glorify the God and Father of our Lord Jesus Christ:

Concluding with either

and the blessing of God almighty,
the Father, the Son, and the Holy Spirit,
be among you and remain with you always. **Amen.**

Or

and the blessing of God,
creator and redeemer,
giver of life and love,
be with you all, now and for ever. **Amen.**

Or

The Lord bless you and keep you.
The Lord make his face to shine on you
   and be gracious to you.
The Lord lift up his countenance on you,
and give you peace. **Amen.**

19. The minister may say

Go in peace to love and serve the Lord.
   In the name of Christ. Amen.

18. 除非有圣餐，婚礼在此以祝福结束。

如果还未签结婚证书，则在此时签署。

但愿赐忍耐安慰的上帝叫你们彼此同心，效法基督耶稣，一心一口荣耀上帝----我们主耶稣基督的父。

以下其中一段作结束

又愿全能的上帝，圣父、圣子、圣灵，所赐的福，降在你们中间，常与你们同在。
阿们。

或

又愿上帝，那赐生命和慈爱的造物主、救赎主所赐的福与你们，从今直到永远。
阿们。

或

又愿主赐福给你、保护你。
愿主使他的脸光照你、赐恩给你。
愿主向你仰脸、赐你平安。
阿们。

19. 主礼

平平安安的去敬爱主、服事主。
奉基督的名。
阿们。

THE HOLY COMMUNION

20. If Holy Communion is to be celebrated, and a Confession and Absolution is desired, the form on page 68 is used.

THE GREETING OF PEACE

21. All stand. The Greeting of Peace is introduced with these or similar words.

We are the body of Christ.

His Spirit is with us.

The priest says

The peace of the Lord be always with you.

And also with you.

22. A hymn may be sung.

THE GREAT THANKSGIVING

23. The priest takes the bread and wine for the communion, places them on the Lord's Table, and says the following or another authorised Prayer of Thanksgiving and Consecration.

[The Lord be with you.
  And also with you.]
Lift up your hearts.
  We lift them to the Lord.
Let us give thanks to the Lord our God.
  It is right to give our thanks and praise.
All glory, honour, thanks and praise
  be given to you, creator of heaven and earth.
When you made us in your image,
  creating us male and female,
  you gave us the gift of marriage.
When sin marred that image
  you healed our brokenness,
  giving your Son to die for us.

圣餐

20. 认罪文

上帝有永恒的慈爱和怜悯,欢迎并邀请罪人来到主的圣桌前。

片刻安静

让我们以耐心和信心,向神承认自己的罪,并祈求祂的赦免。
最慈悲的上帝,我们承认在思想、言语、和行为上,常常得罪了你;应做的不做,不应做的反去做。我们没有尽心爱你;也没有爱人如己。现在我们痛心懊悔,恳求你施怜悯,为了圣子耶稣基督,饶恕我们的已往,扶助我们的现在,引导我们的将来;好叫我们乐意遵行你的旨意,蒙你悦纳,而归荣耀给你的圣名。 阿门。

赦罪文

全能的上帝施恩给你们,藉着我们的主耶稣基督,饶恕你们所犯的罪,增强你们行善的力量,用圣灵的大能,保守你们进入永生。**阿门。**

21. 全体起立。用以下或类似的言语问安。

我们是基督的身体。
祂的灵与我们同在。
上帝的平安常与你同在。
也与你同在。

22. 诗歌

大祝谢文

23. 牧师预备圣餐,可用以下,或其他已授权的祷文祝圣。

主与你们同在。
也与你同在。
你们心里当仰望主。
我们心里仰望主。
我们应当感谢我主上帝。
感谢我主上帝是应当的。

荣耀、尊贵、感谢、赞美都归给你,创造天地的主。
你以自己的形象创造我们,有男有女。你又赐给我们婚姻作礼物。
当罪损坏了这形象时,你赐你的圣子,为我们而死,医治我们的破碎。

Therefore we raise our voices,
>   with all who have served you in every age,
>   to proclaim the glory of your name:
>   **Holy, holy, holy Lord, God of power and might,**
>   **heaven and earth are full of your glory.**
>   **Hosanna in the highest.**
>   **[Blessed is he who comes in the name of the Lord.**
>   **Hosanna in the highest.]**

Most gracious God, we thank you
>   for these gifts of your creation,
>   this bread and wine,
>   and we pray that by your Word and Holy Spirit,
>   we who eat and drink them
>   may be partakers of Christ's body and blood.

On the night he was betrayed Jesus took bread;
>   and when he had given you thanks
>   he broke it, and gave it to his disciples, saying,
>   'Take, eat. This is my body given for you.
>   Do this in remembrance of me.'

After supper, he took the cup,
>   and again giving you thanks
>   he gave it to his disciples, saying,
>   'Drink from this, all of you.
>   This is my blood of the new covenant
>   shed for you and for many
>   for the forgiveness of sins.
>   Do this, as often as you drink it, in remembrance of me.'

The memorial acclamation is used here or below.
>   **Christ has died.**
>   **Christ is risen.**
>   **Christ will come again.**

因此，我们与所有在不同世代中服侍你的仆人们，一同高声宣告你荣耀的圣名：
圣哉、圣哉、圣哉，天地万军的主上帝，
你的荣光充满天地。
奉主名而来的，当受赞美！
在至高之处，亦当称颂主！

恩慈的上帝，我们祝谢这饼和杯。
我们求你，藉着你的道和圣灵的力量，
当我们领受这饼和杯时，就能同享基督的身体和宝血。

主耶稣被卖的那一夜，
拿起饼来，祝谢了，就掰开，分给他的门徒，
说："你们拿这个吃，这是我的身体，
为你们舍的；你们应该这样行，以记念我。"

饭后，他也照样拿起杯来，祝谢了，递给门徒，
说："你们都拿这个喝；
这杯是用我的血所立的新约，
为你们和众人，为赦罪流的。
你们每次喝的时候，应该这样行，以记念我。"

基督曾经受死。
基督现已复活。
基督将要再临。

With this bread and this cup,
> in thanksgiving for the gift of your Son,
> we proclaim his passion and death,
> his resurrection and ascension,
> the outpouring of his Spirit,
> and his presence with his people.

The memorial acclamation may be used here.

Renew us by your Holy Spirit,
> unite us in the body of your Son
> and bring us with all your people
> into the joy of your eternal kingdom;
> through Jesus Christ our Lord,
> with whom and in whom,
> by the power of the Holy Spirit,
> we worship you in songs of never-ending praise:
> **Blessing and honour and glory and power**
> **are yours for ever and ever. Amen.**

24. If the Lord's Prayer has not already been said, it is said here.

As our Saviour Christ has taught us, we are confident to pray,
> **Our Father in heaven,**
> **hallowed be your name,**
> **your kingdom come,**
> **your will be done,**
> **on earth as in heaven.**
>
> **Give us today our daily bread.**
>
> **Forgive us our sins**
> > **as we forgive those who sin against us.**
>
> **Save us from the time of trial**
> > **and deliver us from evil.**
>
> **For the kingdom, the power, and the glory are yours**
> **now and for ever. Amen.**

我们以这饼和杯感谢你赐下圣子耶稣基督,
我们宣扬祂的受难和受死,祂的复活和升天,
祂的灵与祂的子民同在。
求圣灵更新我们,使我们与你的圣子合一,
带领我们和你的子民一同进入你永恒喜乐的国度;
奉我们主基督的名,并在圣灵的团契中,我们敬拜你,永远歌颂赞美你:
颂赞、尊贵、荣耀、权柄全是你的,直到永远。阿们。

24. 如果之前没有颂读主祷文,可在此颂读。

    我们的救主耶稣基督曾经教导我们祷告,说:
    我们在天上的父,
    愿人都尊你的名为圣。
    愿你的国降临。
    愿你的旨意行在地上,
    如同行在天上。
    我们日用的饮食,今日赐给我们。
    饶恕我们的罪,如同我们饶恕得罪我们的人。
    不叫我们遇见试探,救我们脱离凶恶。
    因为国度、权柄、荣耀,全是你的,
    直到永远,阿们。

THE BREAKING OF THE BREAD
AND THE COMMUNION

25. The priest breaks the bread. One of the following may be said.

[We break this bread to share in the body of Christ.]
We who are many are one body in Christ,
for we all share in the one bread.

Or

God of promise, you prepare a banquet for us in your kingdom.
Happy are those who are called to the supper of the Lamb.

26. The priest and other communicants receive the Holy Communion.

The sacrament is given with the following words

The body of our Lord Jesus Christ, which was given for you, preserve your body and soul to everlasting life. Take and eat this in remembrance that Christ died for you, and feed on him in your heart by faith with thanksgiving.

And

The blood of our Lord Jesus Christ, which was shed for you, preserve your body and soul to everlasting life. Drink this in remembrance that Christ's blood was shed for you, and be thankful.

Or, the priest says

[The gifts of God for the people of God.]

Come let us take this holy sacrament of the body and blood of Christ in remembrance that he died for us, and feed on him in our hearts by faith with thanksgiving.

The sacrament is given with the following words, after which the communicant responds, Amen.

The body of Christ [the bread of heaven] keep you in eternal life.
Amen.

The blood of Christ [the cup of salvation] keep you in eternal life.
Amen.

25. 牧师在此擘饼，并读以下其中一段。

我們雖眾，仍属一体，
因为我們都是分享這餅。

或

守约的上帝，你为我们预备了天国的宴席。
喜乐归於被召出席羔羊宴席的人们。

26. 分发圣餐

分发者可说：

我们主耶稣基督的身体，为你而舍，保守你的身体和灵魂进入永生。以感恩和信心领受这饼，记念基督为你受死。

和

我们主耶稣基督的宝血，为你而流，保守你的身体和灵魂进入永生。以感恩的心领受这杯，记念基督为你流血。

或

牧师说：

前来领受这圣礼，以记念耶稣基督为我们而死。以信心和感恩的心前来领受。

分发时可说：

基督的身体（天上的粮），保守你进入永生。
阿们！
基督的宝血（救赎的杯），保守你进入永生。
阿们！

THE SENDING OUT OF GOD'S PEOPLE

27. The priest says one of the following or another suitable prayer.

[Let us pray.]

Most gracious God,

we give you thanks for your tender love

in sending Jesus Christ to come among us,

born of a human mother,

to make the way of the cross to be the way of life.

Pour out the abundance of your blessing

on this man and this woman.

Defend them from every enemy.

Lead them into all peace.

Let their love for each other

be a seal upon their hearts,

a mantle about their shoulders,

and a crown upon their heads.

Bless them in their work and in their companionship;

in their sleeping and in their waking;

in their joys and in their sorrows;

in their life and in their death.

Finally, in your mercy,

bring us all to that table

where your saints feast for ever in your heavenly home. **Amen.**

Or

Almighty God, Lord of the universe,

all love, strength, and understanding come from you;

so direct and govern us in body and soul

that we may strive to live according to your word

and to do everything that is agreeable to your will:

through Jesus Christ our Lord. **Amen.**

差遣

27. 牧师说以下其中一段，或其他合适的祷文。

> 让我们祷告：
> 最慈悲的上帝，我们感谢你差派耶稣基督来到我们当中，
> 以人子的身份，使通往十字架的道路，变成生命的道路。
> 赐下你丰盛的恩典给这对新人。
> 在所有敌人面前保护他们。
> 带领他们进入平安。
> 让他们互相爱护，
> 互相印在彼此心中，
> 如披风围绕在彼此的肩膀上，
> 如冠冕带在彼此的头上。
> 他们工作时、彼此陪伴时；
> 睡眠时、醒来时；
> 喜乐时、伤心时；
> 活着时、死亡时，都赐福他们。
> 最後，求你的怜悯，带领我们去到天国中你的圣徒们永恒的盛宴中。
> **阿们。**

或

> 全能的上帝，宇宙的主，
> 爱、力量和聪明都是从你而来；
> 指引和管理我们的身体和灵魂，使我们可以按着你的话语生活，和做你所喜悦的事。
> 奉我们主耶稣基督的名求。**阿们。**

28. The Blessing

May the God of steadfastness and encouragement
grant you to live in such harmony with one another,
in accord with Christ Jesus,
that together you may with one voice
glorify the God and Father of our Lord Jesus Christ:

Concluding with either

and the blessing of God almighty,
the Father, the Son, and the Holy Spirit,
be among you and remain with you always. **Amen.**

Or

and the blessing of God,
Creator and Redeemer,
giver of life and love,
be with you all, now and for ever. **Amen.**

Or

The Lord bless you and keep you.
The Lord make his face to shine on you
   and be gracious to you.
The Lord lift up his countenance on you,
   and give you peace. **Amen.**

29. The minister may say

Go in peace to love and serve the Lord:
In the name of Christ. Amen.

28. 祝福

但愿赐忍耐安慰的上帝叫你们彼此同心，效法基督耶稣，一心一口荣耀上帝----我们主耶稣基督的父。

以下其中一段作结束

又愿全能的上帝，圣父、圣子、圣灵，所赐的福，降在你们中间，常与你们同在。
阿们。

或

又愿创造和救赎，赐生命和爱的上帝，赐福给你们，从今直到永远。
阿们。

或

愿主赐福你和保守你。
愿主的脸光照你和赐恩给你。
愿主的脸转向你和赐你平安。
阿们。

29. 主礼

平平安安的去敬爱主、服侍主。
奉基督的名。
阿们。

FUNERAL SERVICES AND RESOURCES

BEFORE THE SERVICE

The body is brought in at the beginning of the service, or beforehand, the minister meeting it and saying suitable psalms or sentences of Scripture. When the body is brought to the door of the place for the funeral, the following form may be used.

RECEPTION OF THE BODY

1. The minister says

> We receive the body
> of our dear sister/brother N.
> with confidence in God, the giver of life,
> who raised the Lord Jesus from the dead.

The body is then brought to its place for the service, during which time suitable psalms or sentences of Scripture (such as those printed at ¶ 7 and ¶ 10) may be sung or said.

2. When the body has come to its place, the minister may say

> God our Father,
> by raising Christ your Son you conquered the power of death
> and opened for us the way to eternal life.
> As we remember before you our brother/sister N,
> so we ask your help for all who shall gather in his/her memory.
> Grant us the assurance of your presence and grace,
> by the Spirit you have given us,
> through Jesus Christ our Lord. **Amen.**

3. Silence may be kept.

殡礼和资源
崇拜前

遗体在崇拜开始时，或之前送入礼堂。
主礼接收时诵读合适的诗篇或圣经经文。
当遗体在礼堂门口，准备进入，可用以下礼文。

接收遗体

1. 主礼

    我们以信心，在那位赐生命，并叫主耶稣从死里复活的上帝面前，接收亲爱的弟兄/姐妹　姓名　的遗体。

遗体安放在合适的崇拜地点。在此可诵读合适的诗篇或圣经经文。可参考程序7和10。

2. 当遗体安放好，主礼说：

    上帝我们的天父，
    你使圣子基督复活，战胜死亡的权势，
    并为我们打开通往永生的道路。
    当我们在你面前记念我们的弟兄/姐妹　姓名，
    求你帮助每一位在这里记念他/她的人。
    求圣灵赐我们你的同在和恩典的确据，
    奉我们主耶稣基督的名。**阿们。**

3. 片刻安静

The pall may be used to cover the coffin.

Flowers or similar natural objects may be placed at or on the coffin.

Symbols of the person's life may be placed near or on the coffin.

PLACING OF CHRISTIAN SYMBOLS

4. One or more of the following actions may take place at this or another suitable time in the service.

A lighted [Easter] candle may be placed near the coffin.

The coffin may be sprinkled with water.

A copy of the Scriptures may be placed on or near the coffin.

A cross may be placed on or near the coffin.

These actions may take place in silence, or the following words may be used.

   a **The candle**

      Light immortal,

      you brought life and immortality to light through the gospel.

      May we, with N and all the baptised,

      know the full light of your risen presence. Amen.

   b **Water**

      In the waters of baptism we died with Christ,

      and began to walk in newness of life.

      May we, with N and all the baptised,

      be brought to the fulfilment of your eternal kingdom. Amen.

   c **The Scriptures**

      In life N was nourished by the word of God.

      May Christ greet us, with N, saying:

      Come, blessed of my Father! Amen.

   d **The cross**

      Lord Jesus Christ, you bore our sins on the cross.

      May this cross be a sign to us of your love for N,

      and the forgiveness of her/his sins. Amen.

可用罩布覆盖棺木。

鲜花和其他物件可放在棺木里或棺木上。

摆放象征基督教的物品

4. 以下的一项或多项行动可在此时或崇拜中其他合适的时间进行。

摆放点亮的蜡烛在靠近棺木的地方。

向棺木洒水。

摆放圣经在靠近棺木的地方。

摆放十字架在靠近棺木的地方。

这些行动可以在静默中进行或使用以下祷文。

a 蜡烛
不朽之光，
通过福音，你显示了生命和不朽。
愿我们、和 姓名 ，还有所有已受洗的人，看见你復活同在的榮光。**阿们。**

b 水
藉着洗礼我们与基督同死，
开始了新的生命。
愿我们、和 姓名 ，及所有已受洗的人，蒙你引领，进入你永恒的国度。**阿们。**

c 圣经
在 姓名 的生命中，上帝的话语喂养他。
愿基督对我们和 姓名 说：
来，领受我父的祝福。**阿们。**

d 十字架
主耶稣基督，你在十字架上背负了我们的罪。
愿十字架成为你对 姓名 和我们爱和赦罪的记号。
阿们。

A FUNERAL SERVICE

FOR USE IN A CHURCH BUILDING, FUNERAL CHAPEL, OR AT THE HOME

For the congregation

Human beings have sensed the mystery of death, and the pain of grief, since time immemorial. Every society has developed rites to mark the passage from life through death, and to commemorate the dead. Today we do this through the funeral service, and the rites by which we lay a person's body to rest.

The wounds of grief need time and care to heal. The funeral may help this process, by enabling us to acknowledge our loss, give thanks for the life of the person who has died, make our last farewell, and begin to take up life once more.

Christians believe in God, the source and giver of life. God's good news proclaims Jesus Christ to be our living Lord, who laid down his life for us. He knew death, yet triumphed over it, drawing its sting, and was raised by God to new life. Christians affirm the presence of the Spirit of Christ, who helps us in our weakness. Yet we, with all mortals, still face death. Those who put their trust in Christ share the sufferings of their Lord, even in the midst of God's love and care.

A Christian funeral proclaims the Christian hope in the face of death—Jesus Christ, whose resurrection is the promise of our own.

The service in outline is as follows:

    We gather in the presence of God,

    and remember the person who has died.

    We listen and respond to the word of God,

    and proclaim the death and resurrection of Christ.

    We give thanks for the life now ended,

    and pray for those in need.

    We leave the deceased in God's care,

    and we continue life's journey.

殡礼
在教堂内、殡仪馆或家中使用

向会众说：
死亡对人类来说，是一个奥秘。当有人去世时，总会痛苦悲伤。每个社会都有不同的仪式來标记一个生命的结束，纪念这人的死亡。今天我们通过殡礼，使一个人得安息。

悲痛是需要时间和关怀来医治。殡礼是这过程的一部份，让我们正视我们的失落，并为这失去的生命献上感恩，为他/她作出最後的送别。然後，继续我们生命的旅程。

基督徒相信上帝，是赐生命的主。上帝的好消息宣告耶稣基督是我们永活的主。他为我们舍去性命。他知道死亡，却胜过死亡，除去死亡的毒钩。上帝使他从死里复活，有全新的生命。基督徒确信基督的灵与我们同在，我们软弱时帮助我们。现在我们雖然活在世上，仍要面对死亡。那些信靠基督的人，即使在上帝的爱和看顾下，仍在基督里一同承受痛苦。
基督教的殡礼宣告当基督徒面对死亡时，我们在基督耶稣里有盼望。他的复活就是我们的确据。

殡礼的主要程序是：
我们在上帝面前聚集，一同记念故人。
我们聆听和回应上帝的话语，宣扬基督的受死和复活。
我们为一个生命的结束献上感恩，并为有需要的人祷告。
我们将故人交托在上帝手中，继续人生的旅程。

GATHERING IN GOD'S NAME

5. The minister greets the congregation.

> Grace and peace from the Lord be with you.
> **And also with you.**

The minister may continue with these or similar words.

> We have come together
> > to thank God for the life of N,
> > to mourn and honour him/her,
> > to lay to rest his/her mortal body,
> and to support one another in grief.
> We face the certainty of our own death and judgement.
> Yet Christians believe that those who die in Christ
> > share eternal life with him.
> Therefore in faith and hope we turn to God,
> > who created and sustains us all.

6. A hymn, anthem or canticle may be said or sung, or music may be played.

7. The following is said or sung.

> 'I am the resurrection and the life,' says the Lord.
> 'Those who believe in me, even though they die, yet will they live.'
>
> John 11.25

One or more of these (or other sentences of Scripture) may be read.

> The steadfast love of the Lord never ceases,
> his mercies never come to an end;
> they are new every morning; great is your faithfulness.
>
> Lamentations 3.22–23

> As we come forth naked from our mother's womb,
> so shall we go again, naked as we came.
> We shall take nothing for our toil,
> which we may carry away.
> This also is a grievous ill: just as we came, so shall we go.
>
> Ecclesiastes 5.15–16

奉上帝的名聚会

5. 主礼向会众问安。

> 主的恩典与平安常与你们同在。
> **也与你同在。**

主礼继续以下或类似的言语。

> 我们相聚在一起，为<u>姓名</u>的生命感恩，
> 表扬和悼念他/她，
> 使他/她的肉体得安息，
> 并在悲伤中互相扶持。
> 我们知道自己必须要面对死亡和审判。
> 然而，基督徒相信在基督里死亡，会与他一起进入永生。
> 因此，我们把信心和盼望，都转向那位创造并看顾我们的上帝。

6. 诗歌

7. 读以下经文。

> 耶穌對她說：「復活在我，生命也在我。信我的人，雖然死了，也必復活。」（约11:25）

可再读以下或其他经文。

> 我们不致消灭，是出于耶和华诸般的慈爱，是因他的怜悯不至断绝。 23 每早晨这都是新的，你的诚实极其广大。
>
> （哀3:22-23）
>
> 他怎样从母胎赤身而来，也必照样赤身而去，他所劳碌得来的，手中分毫不能带去。 16 他来的情形怎样，他去的情形也怎样，这也是一宗大祸患。
>
> （传5:15-16）

God is our refuge and strength, a very present help in trouble.

Psalm 46.1

Out of the depths I cry to you, O Lord. Lord, hear my voice!
Let your ears be attentive to the voice of my supplications!

Psalm 130.1

God so loved the world that he gave his only Son,
so that everyone who believes in him may not perish
but may have eternal life

John 3.16

What no eye has seen, nor ear heard, nor the human heart conceived, God has prepared for those who love him.

1 Corinthians 2.9

Christ must reign until he has put all his enemies under his feet. The last enemy to be destroyed is death.

1 Corinthians 15.25–26

I am convinced that neither death, nor life,
   nor angels, nor rulers,
   nor things present, nor things to come,
   nor powers, nor height, nor depth,
   nor anything else in all creation,
   will be able to separate us from the love of God
in Christ Jesus our Lord.

Romans 8.38–39

8. The people may join with the minister in saying

[Let us pray.]
Loving God, you alone are the source of life.
May your life-giving Spirit flow through us,
and fill us with compassion, one for another.
In our sorrow give us the calm of your peace.
Kindle our hope, and let our grief give way to joy;
through Jesus Christ our Lord. Amen.

上帝是我们的避难所,是我们的力量,是我们在患难中随时的帮助。
（诗46:1）

耶和华啊,我从深处向你求告。主啊,求你听我的声音！愿你侧耳听我恳求的声音！
（诗130:1-2）

上帝爱世人,甚至将他的独生子赐给他们,叫一切信他的不致灭亡,反得永生。
（约3:16）

上帝为爱他的人所预备的,是眼睛未曾看见,耳朵未曾听见,人心也未曾想到的。
（林前2:9）

因为基督必要做王,等神把一切仇敌都放在他的脚下。 尽末了所毁灭的仇敌就是死。
（林前15:25-26）

因为我深信：无论是死,是生,是天使,是掌权的,是有能的,是现在的事,是将来的事, 是高处的,是低处的,是别的受造之物,都不能叫我们与神的爱隔绝；这爱是在我们的主基督耶稣里的。
（罗8:38-39）

8. 会众可加入主礼一起说：

【让我们一同祷告】
慈爱的上帝,你是生命唯一的源头。
愿你赐生命的灵充满我们,使我们能互相安慰。
在我们的悲伤中,赐给我们平安。
燃点我们的盼望,使喜乐代替忧伤；
奉我们主耶稣基督的名祷告。阿们。

9. A member of the family or a friend may speak about the person who has died. Members of the family and congregation may be invited to place flowers or symbols on or near the coffin. A period of silence and/or music may follow.

10. One or more psalms is said or sung. The response [R] may be used where marked.

    Psalm 23
        [R] I will fear no evil, for you are with me
    The Lord is my shepherd:
        therefore can I lack nothing.
    He shall make me lie down in green pastures:
        and lead me beside still waters. [R]
    He shall refresh my soul:
        and guide me in right pathways for his name's sake.
    Though I walk through the valley of the shadow of death
    I will fear no evil:
        for you are with me;
        your rod and your staff comfort me. [R]
    You spread a table before me
    in the presence of those who trouble me:
        you have anointed my head with oil and my cup shall be full.
    Surely your goodness and loving-kindness will follow me
        all the days of my life:
        and I shall dwell in the house of the Lord for ever. [R]

    From Psalm 90
    [R] Teach us rightly to number our days
    Lord, you have been our refuge:
        from one generation to another.
    Before the mountains were brought forth,
    or the earth and the world were born:
        from everlasting to everlasting you are God. [R]
    You turn us back to dust:
        and say, 'Go back, you children of earth'.
    For a thousand years in your sight
    are as yesterday when it is past:
        or like a watch in the night. [R]

9. 家人或朋友可述说死者生平。

10. 读一篇或更多的诗篇,可用启应方式。

诗篇 23
(应)我雖然行過死蔭的幽谷,也不怕遭害,因為你與我同在。

(启) 耶和华是我的牧者,
　　我必不致缺乏。
　　他使我躺卧在青草地上,
(应) 领我在可安歇的水边。
(启) 他使我的灵魂苏醒,
　　为自己的名引导我走义路。
　　我虽然行过死荫的幽谷,
　　也不怕遭害
　　因为你与我同在,
(应) 你的杖、你的竿都安慰我。
(启) 在我敌人面前,你为我摆设筵席,
　　你用油膏了我的头,使我的福杯满溢。
　　我一生一世必有恩惠、慈爱随着我,
(应) 我且要住在耶和华的殿中,直到永远。

诗篇 90
(应) 求你指教我们怎样数算自己的日子,

(启) 主啊,你世世代代做我们的居所。
诸山未曾生出,
　　地与世界你未曾造成,
(应) 从亘古到永远,你是上帝。
(启) 你使人归于尘土,说:
　　「你们世人要归回」
　　在你看来,千年如已过的昨日,
(应) 又如夜间的一更。

You cut them off like a dream:
> and like the new grass of the morning.

In the morning it springs up and flourishes:
> in the evening it is dried up and withered. [R]

When you are angry, all our days pass away:
> we bring our years to an end like a sigh.

The span of our life is seventy years,
or, if we have strength, perhaps eighty:
> yet the pride of our toil is but trouble and sorrow,
> for it passes away quickly and we are gone. [R]

Who knows the power of your wrath?:
> who knows your indignation like those who fear you?

Teach us rightly to number our days:
> so that we may apply our hearts to wisdom. [R]

Psalm 121

[R] My help comes from the Lord

I lift my eyes to the hills:
> from where is my help to come?

My help comes from the Lord:
> the maker of heaven and earth. [R]

The Lord will not allow your foot to slip:
> your guardian will not sleep.

See, the one who watches over Israel:
> shall neither slumber nor sleep. [R]

It is the Lord who is your keeper:
> the Lord is your shelter on your right hand,

So that the sun shall not strike you by day:
> neither shall the moon by night. [R]

The Lord shall preserve you from all evil:
> it is the Lord who shall guard your life.

The Lord shall watch over your going out and your coming in:
> both now and for evermore. [R]

Other suitable psalms include:

Psalm 46; Psalm 71; Psalm 130 (in Funeral for a Child); Psalm 139.1–11 (in Funeral for an Infant).

（启）你叫他们如水冲去，他们如睡一觉。
　　早晨他们如生长的草，早晨发芽生长，
（应）晚上割下枯干。
（启）我们因你的怒气而消灭，
　　因你的愤怒而惊惶。
　　你将我们的罪孽摆在你面前，
将我们的隐恶摆在你面光之中。
我们经过的日子都在你震怒之下，
我们度尽的年岁好像一声叹息。
我们一生的年日是七十岁，若是强壮可到八十岁，
但其中所矜夸的不过是劳苦愁烦；
（应）转眼成空，我们便如飞而去。
（启）谁晓得你怒气的权势？
　　谁按着你该受的敬畏晓得你的愤怒呢？
　　求你指教我们怎样数算自己的日子，
（应）好叫我们得着智慧的心。

诗篇121

（应）我的帮助从耶和华而来。
（启）我要向山举目。
　　我的帮助从何而来？
　　我的帮助
（应）从造天地的耶和华而来。
（启）他必不叫你的脚摇动，
　　保护你的必不打盹。
　　保护以色列的
（应）也不打盹，也不睡觉。
（启）保护你的是耶和华，
　　耶和华在你右边荫庇你。
　　白日，太阳必不伤你；
（应）夜间，月亮必不害你。
（启）耶和华要保护你免受一切的灾害，
　　他要保护你的性命。
　　你出你入，耶和华要保护你，
（应）从今时直到永远。

其他合适的诗篇有：46, 71, 130 (儿童殡礼), 139:1-11 (婴儿殡礼)。

THE MINISTRY OF THE WORD

11. One or more of the following readings is read, or some other suitable passages from Scripture.

Romans 6.3–9

Do you not know that all of us who have been baptised
    into Christ Jesus were baptised into his death?
Therefore we have been buried with him by baptism into death, so that, just as Christ was raised from the dead
    by the glory of the Father,
    so we too might walk in newness of life.
For if we have been united with him in a death like his,
we will certainly be united with him in a resurrection like his.
We know that our old self was crucified with him
    so that the body of sin might be destroyed,
    and we might no longer be enslaved to sin.
For whoever has died is freed from sin.
But if we have died with Christ,
    we believe that we will also live with him.
We know that Christ, being raised from the dead,
    will never die again;
    death no longer has dominion over him.

1 Corinthians 15.50b–58

Flesh and blood cannot inherit the kingdom of God,
    nor does the perishable inherit the imperishable.
Listen, I will tell you a mystery!
We will not all die, but we will all be changed, in a moment,
    in the twinkling of an eye, at the last trumpet.
For the trumpet will sound,
    and the dead will be raised imperishable,
    and we will be changed.
For this perishable body must put on the imperishable,
    and this mortal body must put on immortality.
When this perishable body puts on the imperishable,
    and this mortal body puts on immortality,
then the saying that is written will be fulfilled:

圣言职事

11. 读以下一段或更多，或其他合适的经文。

罗6:3-9
岂不知我们这受洗归入基督耶稣的人，是受洗归入他的死吗？所以，我们借着洗礼归入死，和他一同埋葬，原是叫我们一举一动有新生的样式，像基督借着父的荣耀从死里复活一样。我们若在他死的形状上与他联合，也要在他复活的形状上与他联合。因为知道，我们的旧人和他同钉十字架，使罪身灭绝，叫我们不再做罪的奴仆，因为已死的人是脱离了罪。我们若是与基督同死，就信必与他同活。因为知道，基督既从死里复活，就不再死，死也不再做他的主了。

林前15:50b-58
血肉之体不能承受神的国，
必朽坏的不能承受不朽坏的。
我如今把一件奥秘的事告诉你们：
我们不是都要睡觉，乃是都要改变，
就在一霎时，眨眼之间，号筒末次吹响的时候。
因号筒要响，死人要复活成为不朽坏的，
我们也要改变。
这必朽坏的总要变成不朽坏的，
这必死的总要变成不死的。
这必朽坏的既变成不朽坏的，这必死的既变成不死的，
那时经上所记「死被得胜吞灭」的话就应验了。

'Death has been swallowed up in victory.'

'Where, O death, is your victory?

Where, O death, is your sting?'

The sting of death is sin, and the power of sin is the law.

But thanks be to God, who gives us the victory

through our Lord Jesus Christ.

Therefore, my beloved, be steadfast, immovable,

always excelling in the work of the Lord,

because you know that in the Lord your labour is not in vain.

John 14.1–6

Jesus said, 'Do not let your hearts be troubled. Believe in God, believe also in me. In my Father's house there are many dwelling places. If it were not so, would I have told you that I go to prepare a place for you? And if I go and prepare a place for you, I will come again and will take you to myself, so that where I am, there you may be also. And you know the way to the place where I am going.'

Thomas said to him, 'Lord, we do not know where you are going. How can we know the way?'

Jesus said to him, 'I am the way, and the truth and the life. No one comes to the Father except through me.'

Other suitable passages include:
Romans 8.31–38 God's love in Christ Jesus
1 Corinthians 13 Faith, hope and love
1 Corinthians 15 The resurrection of the dead
2 Corinthians 4.16–5.10 Living by faith and hope
Philippians 3.10–16, 20–21 God's purposes for us
1 Thessalonians 4.13–18 The coming of the Lord
Revelation 21.1–7 The new heaven and the new earth
Matthew 5.1–12a True happiness
John 6.35–40 Jesus the Bread of life, who raises us up
John 11.17–27 Jesus the Resurrection and the Life
John 20.11–18 Mary encounters the risen Jesus

死啊，你得胜的权势在哪里？死啊，你的毒钩在哪里？」
死的毒钩就是罪，罪的权势就是律法。
感谢上帝，使我们借着我们的主耶稣基督得胜！
所以，我亲爱的弟兄们，你们务要坚固，
不可摇动，常常竭力多做主工，
因为知道，你们的劳苦在主里面不是徒然的。

约14:1-6
「你们心里不要忧愁，你们信神，也当信我。
在我父的家里有许多住处，若是没有，我就早已告诉你们了，我去原是为你们预备地方去。
我若去为你们预备了地方，就必再来接你们到我那里去，我在哪里，叫你们也在哪里。
我往哪里去你们知道，那条路你们也知道。」
多马对他说：「主啊，我们不知道你往哪里去，怎么知道那条路呢？」
耶稣说：「我就是道路、真理、生命。若不借着我，没有人能到父那里去。」

其他合适的经文有：

罗8:31-38

林前13

林前15

林後4:16-5:10

腓3:10-16, 20-21

帖前4:13-18

启21:1-7

太5:1-12a

约6:35-40

约11:17-27

约20:11-18

12. The Sermon

A period of silence may follow.

13. The following or another hymn may be used.

From The Song of the Church (Te Deum Laudamus)
>You, Lord Christ, are the King of glory:
>the eternal Son of the Father.

When you took our flesh to set us free:
>you humbly chose the Virgin's womb.

You overcame the sting of death:
>and opened the kingdom of heaven to all believers.

You are seated at God's right hand in glory:
>We believe that you will come to be our judge.

Come then, Lord, and help your people,
bought with the price of your own blood:
>and bring us with your saints to glory everlasting.
>even so in Christ shall all be made alive.

12. 讲道

安静片刻

13. 赞美颂

 基督是有荣耀的君王。
  是圣父无始无终的圣子。
  主要救世的人,甘心卑贱,为童贞女所生。
  主既胜了死的苦楚,就是为了一切信道的人,开了天国的门。
  主坐在天主的右边,与圣父一同受荣耀。
  我们信主必再降临,审判我们。
  所以求主救护主的仆婢,就是主用宝贝的血所救赎的。
  叫他们列在圣徒的中间,同享无穷尽的荣耀。

THE PRAYERS

14. The minister says

Let us pray with confidence to God our Father,
who raised Jesus Christ from the dead for the salvation of all.
Thanksgiving
Thanks be to God for the gift of life.
You have made us in your image,
and called us to reflect your truth and light.
We thank you for the life of N.
> We give thanks for N's
> family life and friends...
> contribution to the community...
> commitment to work ...
> leisure activities and other interests...
> personal qualities...
> strength in adversity...
> faith, love and hope...
> ministries in the Church...

Above all, we thank you for your gracious promise
to all your servants, living and departed,
that we shall be made one again
in our Lord Jesus Christ. **Amen.**

And/or

Gracious God, Father, Son and Holy Spirit,
we thank you that you received N by baptism
into the family of your Church on earth,
and granted her/him the gift of eternal life.
S/he ate with us the bread of life
and drank from the cup of salvation.
We thank you for all your goodness to N,
in Christ our Saviour. **Amen.**

Other prayers of thanksgiving may be substituted. An Easter collect, or one of the Prayers of Thanksgiving for the Victory of Christ, is appropriate.

祷告

14. 主礼说：

为了救赎全人类，上帝使耶稣基督从死里复活。让我们以信心向父神祷告。

感恩

感谢赐生命的主。

你以你的形象造我们，并呼召我们反映你的真理和亮光。

我们为 姓名 的生命献上感恩。

> 我们为 姓名 的：
> 家庭和朋友…
> 对社会的贡献…
> 对工作的投入…
> 个人的爱好和兴趣…
> 个人品格…
> 面对逆境的能力…
> 信、望和爱…
> 教会服侍…
> 生活感恩。

最重要的，我们感谢你对你所有仆人的应许，包括在世和已经去世的。你应许我们在基督里将会再次的合而为一。

或/和

恩慈的上帝，圣父、圣子、圣灵，
我们感谢你透过洗礼使 姓名 加入你在地上的教会，并赐给他/她永生作礼物。
他/她曾与我们一同分享生命的饼，和喝救恩的杯。
我们感谢你向 姓名 所施的一切恩惠。
奉主耶稣基督的名求。**阿们。**

也可用其他祷文代替以上祷告。

For those who mourn

God of all mercy, giver of all comfort:
> look graciously, we pray, on those who mourn *especially*...

Casting all their cares on you,
may they know the consolation of your love;
> through Jesus Christ our risen Lord. **Amen.**

Or

Merciful God,
we pray for N's family and friends,
remembering especially ...
whose sense of loss is so keen.
When we cannot understand the things that happen,
> and are weighed down by grief and loneliness,
> uphold us in your love.

Give us the assurance of your constant care,
that we may have courage for the days ahead.
through Jesus Christ our friend. Amen.

Additional prayers may be offered.

Or

15. **The following litany may be used, especially where the Holy Communion follows.**

We thank you, our Father,
that your Son Jesus Christ came to die for us.
We thank you that you raised him from the dead.
We thank you for the gift of life, and the life of N.
Bring us, with N and all your faithful people,
to the fullness of life you promise to those who love you.
Lord, in your mercy
> **hear our prayer.**

We confess that we have not loved you with our whole heart.
We have not loved our neighbours as ourselves.
We repent, and are sorry for all our sins.
Grant us forgiveness, and assure us of your love.
Lord, in your mercy
hear our prayer.

为哀伤的人
赐平安和怜悯的上帝：
求你看顾那些正在哀伤中的人，特别是…
让他们定睛於你，知道你的爱能安慰他们。
奉复活的主耶稣基督名求。**阿们。**

或

慈悲的上帝，我们为 姓名 的家人和朋友祷告，
特别记念…
他们失去了最亲爱的人。
当我们不明白为什麽这些事情会发生，导致我们在痛苦和孤单时，
求你以你的爱来支持我们。
给我们确据知道你你不断看顾我们，
使我们有勇气去面对往後的日子。
奉耶稣基督，我们亲爱的朋友的名求。**阿们。**

可另加祷文。

或

15. 若有圣餐，可用以下祷文。

天父，我们感谢你，
因你的爱子耶稣基督为我们而死。
我们感谢你使他从死里复活。
我们为 姓名 的生命感谢你。
带领我们，和 姓名 ，还有所有忠心的子民，进入你应许给所有爱你的人，那完全的生命中。
求主怜悯。
垂听我们的祷告。
我们承认我们没有全心爱你。我们也没有爱人如己。
我们承认自己的罪，并愿意悔改。
求主赦免我们，并叫我们知道你爱我们。
求主怜悯。
垂听我们的祷告

Strengthen us to love and obey you,
that we may live the rest of our lives in following your Son,
and be ready when you call us to the fullness of eternal life.
Lord, in your mercy
> hear our prayer.

We pray for those who mourn.
Be close to them in their loss.
Increase their faith in your undying love.
Lord, in your mercy
> **hear our prayer.**

Show your mercy to the dying.
Sustain them with hope,
and fill them with the peace and joy of your presence.
Lord, in your mercy
> **hear our prayer.**

We praise you, Lord God, for your faithful servants
in every age.
May we, with [N and] all who have died in the faith of Christ,
be brought to a joyful resurrection
and the fulfilment of your eternal kingdom.
Amen.

16. **If the Lord's Prayer is not to be used at ¶ 17c, the minister continues**

As our Saviour Christ has taught us, we are confident to pray,

> **Our Father in heaven,**
> **hallowed be your name,**
> **your kingdom come,**
> **your will be done,**
> **on earth as in heaven.**
> **Give us today our daily bread.**
> **Forgive us our sins**
> **as we forgive those who sin against us.**
> **Save us from the time of trial**
> **and deliver us from evil.**
> **For the kingdom, the power, and the glory are yours**
> **now and for ever. Amen.**

17. **If the Holy Communion is to be celebrated, please turn to page 222.**

赐我们力量去爱你，顺服你，使我们的余生能跟随你的圣子，
并随时预备你呼召我们进入完全而永恒的生命中。
求主怜悯。
垂听我们的祷告。

我们为在悲伤中的人祷告。
在他们失落中，求你亲近他们。增强他们对你永恒的爱的信心。

求主怜悯。
垂听我们的祷告。

求你怜悯正面对死亡的人。使他们充满盼望，并在你面前满有平安喜乐。

求主怜悯。
垂听我们的祷告。

我主上帝，我们为历代忠心爱你的仆人而赞美你。
求主带领我们，和　姓名　，并所有在基督里死亡的人，进入喜乐的复活和你永恒的国度中。**阿们。**

16. 如果没有圣餐，主礼在这里读主祷文。

    我们的救主耶稣基督曾教导我们这样祷告：
    我们在天上的父，
    愿人都尊你的名为圣。
    愿你的国降临。
    愿你的旨意行在地上，
    如同行在天上。
    我们日用的饮食，今日赐给我们。
    饶恕我们的罪，如同我们饶恕得罪我们的人。
    不叫我们遇见试探，救我们脱离凶恶。
    因为国度、权柄、荣耀，全是你的，
    直到永远，阿们。

17. 如果有圣餐，请转至223页圣餐程序。

THE FAREWELL

18. A hymn may be sung.

19. The minister may say the following or other prayers.

> Lord Jesus Christ, you gave new birth to our brother/sister N
> by water and the Spirit.
> Grant that his/her death may recall to us
> your victory over death,
> and be an occasion for us
> to renew our trust in your Father's love.
> Give us, we pray, the faith to follow
> where you have led the way,
> to live and reign with the Father and the Holy Spirit,
> to the ages of ages. **Amen.**

20. The minister says

Let us entrust our sister/brother N to the mercy of God.

Silence may be kept.

> Holy and loving Father,
> by your mighty power you gave us life,
> and in your love you have given us new life
>> in Christ Jesus.
>
> We entrust N to your merciful keeping:
> in the faith of Jesus Christ,
> who died and rose again to save us,
> and now lives and reigns with you
> and the Holy Spirit
> in glory for ever. **Amen.**

送别

18. 诗歌

19. 主礼读以下，或其他的祷文。

主耶稣基督，你曾经用水和圣灵，使我们的兄弟/姐妹　姓名　得着新的生命。
让他/她的死亡提醒我们，你已经战胜死亡。
这是一个机会让我们更新对父神的爱的信靠。
赐我们信心去跟随你要带领我们走的路，
在圣父和圣灵的掌权下生活，直到万代。
阿们。

20. 主礼说：

让我们把我们的弟兄/姐妹　姓名　交托在上帝的怜悯中。

安静片刻

圣洁和慈爱的父神，
因着你的大能，你赐给我们生命。
在耶稣基督里，因着你的爱，你又赐给我们新的生命。
我们把　姓名　交托在你恩手中：
奉那位曾经为拯救我们而受死、复活，
现在与你和圣灵一同在永恒的荣耀中、
掌权的耶稣基督的名求。
阿们。

THE COMMITTAL

21. The committal of the body may take place at this point, if it is not to occur at the graveside or crematorium.

Facing the coffin, the minister says

> Almighty God, our heavenly Father,
> you have given us a sure and certain hope
>> of the resurrection to eternal life.
> In your keeping are all who have departed in Christ.
> We here commit the body of our dear brother/sister N
>> to be cremated
>> to the deep
>> to be buried in the ground,
> in the name of our Lord Jesus Christ,
> who died, and was buried, and rose again for us,
> and who shall change our mortal body
> that it may be like his glorious body.

The congregation may join with the minister

> **Thanks be to God who gives us the victory
> through Jesus Christ our Lord. Amen.**

Other prayers may be added.

安葬礼

21. 如果安葬礼不在坟场或火葬场举行，则可在此举行。

面对棺木，主礼说：

全能的上帝，我们天上的父，
你给了我们有复活和永生的确据。
能在基督里离开世界是因为你的保守。
现在我们将亲爱的弟兄/姐妹 姓名，

　火化，

　埋葬，

奉那位曾经为我们受死、埋葬和复活，
也能将我们从必死的身体变成像他荣耀的身体一样的主耶稣基督的名。

会众与主礼一起说：

感谢那位藉着我们主耶稣基督赐给我们得胜的上帝。阿们。

可加入其他祷告。

THE BLESSING AND DISMISSAL

22. The minister says

The grace of the Lord Jesus Christ, and the love of God,
and the fellowship of the Holy Spirit,
be with us all evermore. **Amen.**

Or the priest says

The Lord bless you and keep you;
The Lord make his face to shine upon you,
    and be gracious to you.
The Lord lift up his countenance upon you,
    and give you peace. **Amen.**

The minister may say

Go in peace in the name of Christ. Amen.

23. As the body is carried out, a hymn, or one or more of these anthems, may be sung or said.

Christ is risen from the dead, trampling down death by death,
    and giving life to those in the tomb.
The Sun of Righteousness is gloriously risen,
    giving light to those who sat in darkness
    and in the shadow of death.
Christ will open the kingdom of heaven
    to all who believe in him, saying,
Come, O blessed of my Father;
    inherit the kingdom prepared for you.

And/or

Lord now you let your servant go in peace:
your word has been fulfilled.
My own eyes have seen the salvation:
which you have prepared in the sight of every people;
a light to reveal you to the nations:
and the glory of your people Israel.

Luke 2.29–32

祝福和散会

22. 主礼

愿主耶稣基督的恩惠，上帝的慈爱，圣灵的感动交通，常与我们同在。
阿们。

或牧师说：

願耶和華賜福給你，保護你。
願耶和華使他的臉光照你，賜恩給你。
願耶和華向你仰臉，賜你平安。
阿们。

主礼可说：

你们要奉主的名平平安安的离去。**阿们。**

23. 当遗体被送出时，可唱诗歌，或读以下经文。

主啊，如今可以照你的话，
释放仆人安然去世！
因为我的眼睛已经看见你的救恩，
就是你在万民面前所预备的，
是照亮外邦人的光，
又是你民<u>以色列</u>的荣耀。
（路2:29-32）

THE HOLY COMMUNION ON THE DAY OF A FUNERAL

THE GREETING OF PEACE

17a. All stand. The Greeting of Peace is introduced with these or other suitable words.

We are the body of Christ.
His Spirit is with us.

The priest says

The peace of the Lord be always be with you.
And also with you.

THE GREAT THANKSGIVING

17b. The priest takes the bread and wine for the communion, places them on the Lord's Table, and says this or another authorised Prayer of Thanksgiving and Consecration.

[The Lord be with you
And also with you.]
Lift up your hearts.
We lift them to the Lord.
Let us give thanks to the Lord our God.
It is right to give our thanks and praise.
Blessed are you, gracious God,
creator of heaven and earth,
giver of life, and conqueror of death.
By his death on the cross,
your Son Jesus Christ
offered the one true sacrifice for sin,
breaking the power of evil
and putting death to flight.
With all your saints
we give you thanks and praise.

殡礼中的圣餐
问安

17a. 全体起立。可用以下，或合适的话语问安。

> 我们是基督的身体。
> **他的灵与我们同在。**

牧师说：

> 愿主的平安常与你们同在。
> **也与你同在。**

会众互相问安。

大祝谢文

17b. 预备圣餐的饼和酒。牧师用以下或其他授权礼文作感恩和祝圣祷告。

> 主与你们同在。
> > **也与你同在。**
>
> 你们心里当仰望主。
> > **我们心里仰望主。**
>
> 我们应当感谢我主上帝。
> > **感谢我主上帝是应当的。**
>
> 恩慈的上帝
> 赞美归於你，
> 你创造天地，赐生命，并战胜死亡。
> 因着你的圣子耶稣基督在十字架上的受死，
> 为罪一次献上了完全的赎罪祭，
> 打破了魔鬼的权势，
> 战胜了死亡。
> 我们与众圣徒一起向你献上感谢和赞美。

Through his resurrection from the dead
> you have given us new birth into a living hope,
> into an inheritance which is imperishable,
> undefiled, and unfading.

With all your saints
> we give you thanks and praise.

The joy of resurrection fills the universe,
> and so we join with angels and archangels,
> with [N and] all your faithful people,
> evermore praising you and saying,

Holy, holy, holy Lord, God of power and might.
Heaven and earth are full of your glory.
Hosanna in the highest.
[Blessed is he who comes in the name of the Lord.
Hosanna in the highest.]

Merciful God, we thank you
> for these gifts of your creation,
> this bread and wine,
> and we pray that by your Word and Holy Spirit,
> we who eat and drink them
> may be partakers of Christ's body and blood.

On the night he was betrayed Jesus took bread;
> and when he had given you thanks
> he broke it, and gave it to his disciples, saying,
> 'Take, eat. This is my body given for you.
> Do this in remembrance of me.'

After supper, he took the cup,
> and again giving you thanks
> he gave it to his disciples, saying,
> 'Drink from this, all of you.
> This is my blood of the new covenant
> shed for you and for many
> for the forgiveness of sins.
> Do this, as often as you drink it, in remembrance of me.'

The memorial acclamation is used here or below.

通过他的死里复活，
你赐给我们新生命中的盼望，
好得到不朽壞、不玷污、不衰殘的基業。
我们与众圣徒一起向你献上感谢和赞美。

你复活的喜乐充满宇宙，
因此，我们和天使与天使长，并 姓名 ，
和所有你忠心的子民，
一同永远赞美你，说：

圣哉、圣哉、圣哉，天地万军的主上帝，
你的荣光充满天地。
奉主名而来的，当受赞美！
在至高之处，亦当称颂主！

慈悲的上帝，我们祝谢这饼和酒。
我们求你，藉着你的道和圣灵的力量，
当我们领受这饼和杯时，
我们可以与基督的身体和宝血联合。

主耶稣被卖的那一夜，
拿起饼来，祝谢了，就擘开，分给他的门徒，
说："你们拿这个吃，这是我的身体，
为你们舍的；你们应该这样行，以记念我。"

饭后，他也照样拿起杯来，祝谢了，递给门徒，
说："你们都拿这个喝；
这杯是用我的血所立的新约，
为你们和众人，为赦罪流的。
你们每次喝的时候，应该这样行，以记念我。"

Christ has died.
Christ is risen.
Christ will come again.
Therefore with thanksgiving for the gift of your Son
    we here proclaim his passion and death,
        and his victory over the grave.

The memorial acclamation may be used here.

Renew us by your Holy Spirit,
    unite us in the body of your Son
    and bring us with [N and] all your faithful people
    into the joy of your eternal kingdom;
    with whom, in the unity of the Holy Spirit,
    through Jesus Christ our Lord,
    we offer our prayer and praise:
    Blessing and honour and glory and power
    are yours for ever and ever. Amen.

17c. If the Lord's Prayer has not already been said, it is said here or after the Communion.

As our Saviour Christ has taught us, we are confident to pray,
Our Father in heaven,
    hallowed be your name,
    your kingdom come,
    your will be done,
    on earth as in heaven.
Give us today our daily bread.
Forgive us our sins
    as we forgive those who sin against us.
Save us from the time of trial
    and deliver us from evil.
For the kingdom, the power, and the glory are yours,
now and for ever. Amen.

基督曾经受死。
基督现已复活。
基督将要再临。

因此,我们感谢你以圣子作为礼物,
我们在此宣扬他的受难和受死,
并在坟墓中的得胜。

求圣灵更新我们,使我们与你的圣子合一,
带领我们和你的子民一同进入你永恒喜乐的国度;
奉我们主耶稣基督的名,并在圣灵的团契中,
我们敬拜你,永远歌颂赞美你:

颂赞、尊贵、荣耀、权柄全是你的,直到永远。阿们。

17c. 可在此,或圣餐後读主祷文:

我们的救主耶稣基督曾教导我们这样祷告:

**我们在天上的父,
愿人都尊你的名为圣。
愿你的国降临。
愿你的旨意行在地上,
如同行在天上。
我们日用的饮食,今日赐给我们。
饶恕我们的罪,如同我们饶恕得罪我们的人。
不叫我们遇见试探,救我们脱离凶恶。
因为国度、权柄、荣耀,全是你的,
直到永远,阿们。**

THE BREAKING OF THE BREAD AND THE COMMUNION

17d. The priest breaks the bread. The following may be said.

[We break this bread to share in the body of Christ.]

We who are many are one body,

for we all share in the one bread.

17e. The priest and other communicants receive the Holy Communion.

The sacrament is given with the following words.

The body of our Lord Jesus Christ, which was given for you, preserve your body and soul to everlasting life. Take and eat this in remembrance that Christ died for you, and feed on him in your heart by faith with thanksgiving.

And

The blood of our Lord Jesus Christ, which was shed for you, preserve your body and soul to everlasting life. Drink this in remembrance that Christ's blood was shed for you, and be thankful.

Or, the priest says

[The gifts of God for the people of God.]

Come let us take this holy sacrament of the body and blood of Christ in remembrance that he died for us, and feed on him in our hearts by faith with thanksgiving.

The sacrament is given with the following words, after which the communicant responds, Amen.

The body of Christ [the bread of heaven] keep you

in eternal life. **Amen.**

The blood of Christ [the cup of salvation] keep you

in eternal life. **Amen.**

During the communion, psalms, hymns or anthems may be sung or said.

17d. 牧师在此擘饼，并读以下其中一段。

我們虽众，仍属一体，
因为我們都是分享這餅。

17e. 分发圣餐

分发者可说：

我们主耶稣基督的身体，为你而舍，保守你的身体和灵魂进入永生。以感恩和信心领受这饼，记念基督为你受死。

和

我们主耶稣基督的宝血，为你而流，保守你的身体和灵魂进入永生。以感恩的心领受这杯，记念基督为你流血。

或

牧师说：

前来领受这圣礼，以记念耶稣基督为我们而死。以信心和感恩的心前来领受。

分发时可说：

基督的身体（天上的粮），保守你进入永生。**阿们！**
基督的宝血（救恩的杯），保守你进入永生。**阿们！**

领圣餐时可有诗歌

AFTER COMMUNION

17f. The priest may say this or another suitable prayer.

[Let us pray.]

Lord of life and death,

we thank you that in your great love

you have given us this foretaste of the heavenly banquet

    prepared for all your saints.

Grant that this sacrament of Christ's death may be to us

    a comfort in affliction,

    a firm assurance of his resurrection,

    and a pledge of our inheritance in that kingdom

    where death and sorrow are no more,

    but all things are made new. Amen.

The service continues at the Farewell at ¶ 18.

圣餐後礼文

17f. 牧师可读以下或其他合适经文。

让我们一同祷告：

生命和死亡的主，我们感谢你。
在你的大爱中，你预先给我们先尝了你在天堂中为众圣徒所预备的宴席。
愿这记念耶稣受死的圣礼，
成为我们悲痛中的安慰，
他复活的确据，
和承受天国的保证。
在那里没有死亡和痛苦，一切都是新的。
阿们。

回到程序第18。

AT THE GRAVESIDE OR CREMATORIUM

PREPARATION

24. When the body is brought to the place, the minister meets it at the entrance. If appropriate, a hymn may be sung or other music used.

25. The minister greets those who have gathered.

Grace and peace from the Lord be with you.

And also with you.

One or more of these or other appropriate sentences from Scripture may be read.

If we live, we live to the Lord,
    and if we die, we die to the Lord;
so then, whether we live or whether we die, we are the Lord's.
For to this end Christ died and lived again,
so that he might be Lord of both the dead and the living.   Romans 14.8–9

Blessed be the God and Father of our Lord Jesus Christ!
By his great mercy he has given us new birth
    into a living hope
through the resurrection of Jesus Christ from the dead,
and into an inheritance that is imperishable,
    undefiled, and unfading, kept in heaven for you.   1 Peter 1.3–4

For since we believe that Jesus died and rose again,
even so, through Jesus, God will bring with him
those who have fallen asleep.   1 Thessalonians 4.14

We brought nothing into the world—
it is certain that we can take nothing out of it.   1 Timothy 6.7

Naked I came from my mother's womb,
and naked shall I return there;
The Lord gave, and the Lord has taken away;
blessed be the name of the Lord.   Job 1.21

在坟场或火葬场
准备

24. 当遗体进入场地时,主礼在门口迎接。

可唱诗歌

25. 主礼向众人问安。

愿主的恩惠和平安与你们同在。
也与你同在。

可读以下一段或更多的经文。

我们若活着,是为主而活;若死了,是为主而死。所以,我们或活或死,总是主的人。因此基督死了,又活了,为要做死人并活人的主。

(罗14:8-9)

愿颂赞归于我们主耶稣基督的父神!他曾照自己的大怜悯,借着耶稣基督从死里复活,重生了我们,叫我们有活泼的盼望,可以得着不能朽坏、不能玷污、不能衰残、为你们存留在天上的基业。

(彼前1:3-4)

我们若信耶稣死而复活了,那已经在耶稣里睡了的人,神也必将他们与耶稣一同带来。

(帖前4:14)

因为我们没有带什么到世上来,也不能带什么去。

(提前6:7)

我赤身出于母胎,也必赤身归回;赏赐的是耶和华,收取的也是耶和华。耶和华的名是应当称颂的!"

(伯1:21)

THE COMMITTAL

26. The following may be said.

> In the midst of life we are in death.
> We blossom like a flower, and wither.
> We pass like a shadow, and do not stay.
> From whom may we seek for help,
> > but from you, Lord God,
> > > though you are justly grieved on account of our sins?
> Holy and loving Saviour,
> > deliver us from the bitterness of eternal death.
> Keep us, at our last hour, lest we fall from you.

And/or

> You, O Lord, are full of compassion and mercy:
> > slow to anger and of great goodness.
> As a father cares for his children:
> > so is your care, O Lord, for those who fear you.
> For you know of what we are made:
> > you remember that we are but dust.
> Our days are like the grass:
> > we flourish like a flower of the field;
> When the wind goes over it, it is gone:
> > and its place will know it no more.
> But your loving-kindness, O Lord
> > endures for ever and ever
> > > on those that fear you:
> > > > and your righteousness on their children's children.

安葬礼

26. 可读以下礼文。

> 死亡是人生的一部份,
> 我们绽放如花, 随後枯萎。
> 我们像影子一样走过, 不留痕迹。
> 我们可以向谁寻求帮助呢?
> 只有你, 主上帝, 虽然你在为我们的罪而伤心。
> 圣洁和慈爱的救主, 拯救我们脱离永远死亡的痛苦。
> 保守我们最後的时刻, 免得我们跌倒。

和/或

> 主啊, 你是有憐憫, 有恩惠, 不輕易發怒, 且有豐盛的慈愛。
> 父親怎樣憐憫他的兒女,
> 耶和華也怎樣憐憫敬畏他的人!
> 因為他知道我們的本體,
> 思念我們不過是塵土。
> 至於世人, 他的年日如草一樣。
> 他興旺如野地的花,
> 經風一吹, 就歸無有,
> 它的原處也不再認識它。
> 但耶和華的慈愛歸於敬畏他的人,
> 從亙古到永遠;
> 他的公義也歸於子子孫孫。

27. Facing the coffin, and at a burial while earth is cast upon it, the minister says

Almighty God, our heavenly Father,
you have given us a sure and certain hope
of the resurrection to eternal life.
In your keeping are all who have departed in Christ.
We here commit the body of our dear sister/brother N
    to be cremated
    to be buried in the ground,
    earth to earth, ashes to ashes, dust to dust
    to the deep,
in the name of our Lord Jesus Christ,
who died, and was buried, and rose again for us,
and who shall change our mortal body
that it may be like his glorious body.

The congregation may join with the minister

Thanks be to God who gives us the victory
through Jesus Christ our Lord. Amen!

At a burial, family members or friends may be invited to assist in casting earth upon the body, here or at the end of the service.

The minister may continue

Blessed are the dead who die in the Lord,
    for they rest from their labours.

27. 面向棺木，和在入土时，主礼说：

全能的上帝，我们天上的父，
你给了我们在复活和永生上有了确实的盼望。
能在基督里离开世界是因为你的保守。
现在我们将亲爱的弟兄/姐妹　姓名，
　　火化，
埋葬，
尘归尘，土归土
奉那位曾经为我们受死、埋葬和复活，
也能将我们从必死的身体变成像他荣耀的身体一样的主耶稣基督的名。

会众与主礼一起说：

感谢那位藉着我们主耶稣基督赐给我们得胜的上帝。阿们。

在葬礼中，可邀请家人或朋友帮助埋土。
礼仪到止结束。

主礼也可继续说：

在基督里离世的人是蒙福的，因他们在劳苦中得安息。

THE PRAYERS

28. The minister may say

As our Saviour Christ has taught us, we are confident to pray,
Our Father in heaven,
> hallowed be your name,
> your kingdom come,
> your will be done,
> on earth as in heaven.
Give us today our daily bread.
Forgive us our sins
> as we forgive those who sin against us.
Save us from the time of trial
> and deliver us from evil.
For the kingdom, the power, and the glory are yours
now and for ever. Amen.

29. The minister says one or more of these prayers.

God of truth and love,
> give us wisdom and grace
> to use aright the time left to us.
While we have opportunity,
> lead us to repent of our sins,
> and to do what we have left undone.
Strengthen us to follow in the steps of Jesus,
along the pilgrim way to your eternal kingdom;
through Jesus Christ our Lord. **Amen.**
God of all consolation,
> in your unending love and mercy for us
> you turn the darkness of death
into the dawn of new life.
Be our refuge and strength in sorrow.
As your Son, our Lord Jesus Christ,
> by dying for us conquered death,
> and by rising again restored us to life,
> so may we go forward in faith to meet him,

祷告

28. 主礼可说：

我们的救主耶稣基督曾教导我们这样祷告：
我们在天上的父，
愿人都尊你的名为圣。
愿你的国降临。
愿你的旨意行在地上，
如同行在天上。
我们日用的饮食，今日赐给我们。
饶恕我们的罪，如同我们饶恕得罪我们的人。
不叫我们遇见试探，救我们脱离凶恶。
因为国度、权柄、荣耀，全是你的，
直到永远，阿们。

29. 主礼读以下一段或更多的祷文。

真理和慈爱的上帝，
赐给我们智慧和恩典去使用生命中剩下的时间。
当我们仍有机会的时候，带领我们为自己的罪悔改，
并做我们还没有该做的事。
帮助我们跟随耶稣的脚步，
行天路，走向你永恒的国度。
奉我们主耶稣基督的名祷告。**阿们。**

赐一切安慰的上帝，
因着你无尽的慈爱和怜悯，你使死亡的黑暗变成新生命的曙光。
在痛苦中你是我们的保障" 或 "你是我们的避难所和力量。
如你的圣子，我们的救主耶稣基督，
为我们而死，并战胜死亡。
他的复活使我们有新生命。
使我们继续以信心前行，

and after our life on earth

be united with our dear brothers and sisters in Christ

where every tear will be wiped away,

through Jesus Christ our Lord. **Amen.**

Additional prayers may be offered.

30. The minister says one or more of the following.

Now to him who is able to keep you from falling,

and to make you stand without blemish

in the presence of his glory with rejoicing,

to the only God our Saviour, through Jesus Christ our Lord,

be glory, majesty, power and authority,

before all time and now and for ever. **Amen.**

Jude 24–25

The grace of the Lord Jesus Christ,

and the love of God,

and the fellowship of the Holy Spirit, be with us all. **Amen.**

2 Corinthians 13.14

May God in his infinite love and mercy

bring the whole Church,

living and departed in the Lord Jesus,

to a joyful resurrection

and the fulfilment of his eternal kingdom. **Amen.**

The minister may say

Go in peace in the name of Christ. **Amen.**

在我们离世的时候,可以与我们亲爱的弟兄姐妹在基督里再相遇。
在那里,泪水会被擦干,
奉我们主耶稣基督的名。**阿们。**

可加其他祷文

30. 主礼读一段或更多以下的祷文。

   那能保守你们不失脚,
   叫你们无瑕无疵、欢欢喜喜站在他荣耀之前的我们的救主独一的神,
   愿荣耀、威严、能力、权柄
   因我们的主耶稣基督归于他,
   从万古以前并现今,直到永永远远!阿门。
   (犹24-25)

   愿主耶稣基督的恩惠、上帝的慈爱、圣灵的感动,常与你们众人同在!
   (林後13:14)

   愿上帝按他永恒的慈爱和怜悯,使全教会在基督里在世和离世的信徒,进入复活的喜乐,和永恒的天国中。**阿们。**

THE INTERMENT OF THE ASHES

1. The minister greets those who have gathered.

Grace and peace from the Lord be with you.

And also with you.

One or more of the following or other appropriate sentences from Scripture are read.

Jesus said, 'I am the resurrection and the life.
Those who believe in me, even though they die, will live,
and everyone who lives and believes in me will never die.'

John 11.25–26

Christ, being raised from the dead, will never die again;
death no longer has dominion over him.
The death he died, he died to sin, once for all;
but the life he lives, he lives to God.

Romans 6.9–10

I am convinced that neither death, nor life,
nor angels, nor rulers,
nor things present, nor things to come,
nor powers, nor height, nor depth,
nor anything else in all creation,
will be able to separate us from the love of God
in Christ Jesus our Lord.

Romans 8.38–39

Blessed be the God and Father of our Lord Jesus Christ!
By his great mercy he has given us new birth
into a living hope
through the resurrection of Jesus Christ from the dead,
and into an inheritance that is imperishable,
undefiled, and unfading, kept in heaven for you.

1 Peter 1.3–4

骨灰安葬礼

1. 主礼向众人问安。

    愿上帝的恩惠和平安与你们同在。
    也与你同在。

读一段或更多以下的经文。

    耶稣对她说:「复活在我,生命也在我。信我的人,虽然死了,也必复活;凡活着信我的人必永远不死。 」
    (约11:25-26)

    因为知道,基督既从死里复活,就不再死,死也不再做他的主了。
    他死是向罪死了,只有一次;他活是向神活着。
    (罗6:9-10)

    因为我深信: 无论是死,是生,是天使,
    是掌权的,是有能的,
    是现在的事,是将来的事,
    是高处的,是低处的,
    是别的受造之物,
    都不能叫我们与神的爱隔绝;
    这爱是在我们的主基督耶稣里的。
    (罗8:38-39)

    愿颂赞归于我们主耶稣基督的父神!
    他曾照自己的大怜悯,
    借着耶稣基督从死里复活,重生了我们,
    叫我们有活泼的盼望, 可以得着不能朽坏、不能玷污、不能衰残、
    为你们存留在天上的基业。
    (彼前1:3-4)

2. The minister may say

> God our creator, giver of life and all that is good and true,
> we thank you for the life of your servant, N.
> Preserve among us the good of his/her example,
> and keep us in the way of truth,
> until we come to your eternal kingdom;
> through Jesus Christ our Lord. **Amen.**

THE INTERMENT

3. As the ashes are interred in a prepared place, the minister says

> God our Father,
> > in loving care your hand has created us,
> > and as the potter fashions the clay
> > you have formed us in your image.
> Through the Holy Spirit
> > you have breathed into us the gift of life.
> In the sharing of love you have enriched our knowledge
> > of you and of one another.
> We claim your love today,
> > as we commit these remains of N to their resting place,
> > earth to earth, ashes to ashes, dust to dust,
> in sure and certain hope of the resurrection to eternal life.

The congregation may join with the minister in saying

> **Thanks be to God who gives us the victory**
> **through Jesus Christ our Lord. Amen!**

4. The minister reads these verses of Scripture.

> Listen, I will tell you a mystery!
> We will not all fall asleep, but we will all be changed,
> > in a moment, in the twinkling of an eye, at the last trumpet.
> For the trumpet will sound,
> > and the dead will be raised imperishable,
> > and we will be changed.
> For this perishable nature must put on the imperishable,
> and this mortal body must put on immortality.
>
> 1 Corinthians 15.51–53

Other suitable verses may be read.

2. 主礼

    创造万物、赐生命、美善和真理的上帝，
我们为了你的仆人 姓名 的生命献上感恩。
使他/她的好行为，成为我们的榜样，
保守我们在真理的道路上，直到进入你永恒的国度。
奉我们主耶稣基督的名求。**阿们。**

安葬

3. 当骨灰放进预备的地方，主礼说：

    我们的天父，
在你的爱中，你创造了我们。
像陶匠塑造陶泥，你以自己的形象造了我们。
藉着圣灵，你向我们呼出生命的气息。
在你的爱中，你使我们更懂得敬爱你和彼此相爱。
今天我们恳求你的慈爱，
当我们把 姓名 安放在他/她安息之地，尘归尘，土归土时，
确保他/她从复活的盼望中进入永生。

会众可一起说：

    感谢赐我们得胜的上帝。
奉我们主耶稣基督的名求。阿们。

4. 主礼读以下经文。

    我如今把一件奥秘的事告诉你们：
我们不是都要睡觉，乃是都要改变，就在一霎时，眨眼之间，号筒末次吹响的时候。
因号筒要响，死人要复活成为不朽坏的，我们也要改变。
这必朽坏的总要变成不朽坏的，这必死的总要变成不死的。
    （林前15:51-53）

可读其他合适经文。

THE PRAYERS

5. The minister says

As our Saviour Christ has taught us, we are confident to pray,
Our Father in heaven,
   hallowed be your name,
   your kingdom come,
   your will be done,
   on earth as in heaven.
Give us today our daily bread.
Forgive us our sins
   as we forgive those who sin against us.
Save us from the time of trial
   and deliver us from evil.
For the kingdom, the power, and the glory are yours
now and forever. Amen.

The minister continues

God of hope,
grant that we, with all who have believed in you,
may be united in the full knowledge of your love
and the unclouded vision of your glory;
through Jesus Christ our Lord. Amen.

Further prayers may be offered.

6. The minister says one of the following

The grace of the Lord Jesus Christ,
and the love of God,
and the fellowship of the Holy Spirit, be with us all. Amen.

2 Corinthians 13.14

Now to him who is able to keep you from falling,
and to make you stand without blemish
   in the presence of his glory with rejoicing,
to the only God our Saviour, through Jesus Christ our Lord,
be glory, majesty, power and authority,
before all time and now and for ever. Amen.

Jude 24–25

祷告

5. 主礼

   我们的救主耶稣基督曾教导我们这样祷告：
   我们在天上的父，
   愿人都尊你的名为圣。
   愿你的国降临。
   愿你的旨意行在地上，
   如同行在天上。
   我们日用的饮食，今日赐给我们。
   饶恕我们的罪，如同我们饶恕得罪我们的人。
   不叫我们遇见试探，救我们脱离凶恶。
   因为国度、权柄、荣耀，全是你的，
   直到永远，阿们。

主礼继续

   赐盼望的上帝，
   愿我们所有相信你的人，在你的爱中联合，
   清晰看到你的荣耀；奉我们主耶稣基督的名求。**阿们。**

可加其他祷告

6. 主礼说以下其中一段。

   愿主耶稣基督的恩惠、上帝的慈爱、圣灵的感动，常与你们众人同在！
   阿们。
   （林後13:14）
   那能保守你们不失脚，
   叫你们无瑕无疵、欢欢喜喜站在他荣耀之前的我们的救主独一的神，
   愿荣耀、威严、能力、权柄
   因我们的主耶稣基督归于他，
   从万古以前并现今，直到永永远远！阿门。
   （犹24-25）

www.ingramcontent.com/pod-product-compliance
Lightning Source LLC
Chambersburg PA
CBHW020107020526
44112CB00033B/1070